The Peebles Path *to* Real Estate Wealth

How to Make Money in Any Market

R. Donahue Peebles

with **J.P. Faber**

WILEY

John Wiley & Sons, Inc.

Copyright © 2008 by R. Donahue Peebles. All rights reserved.

Published by John Wiley & Sons, Inc., Hoboken, New Jersey.
Published simultaneously in Canada.

No part of this publication may be reproduced, stored in a retrieval system, or transmitted in any form or by any means, electronic, mechanical, photocopying, recording, scanning, or otherwise, except as permitted under Section 107 or 108 of the 1976 United States Copyright Act, without either the prior written permission of the Publisher, or authorization through payment of the appropriate per-copy fee to the Copyright Clearance Center, Inc., 222 Rosewood Drive, Danvers, MA 01923, (978) 750-8400, fax (978) 646-8600, or on the web at www.copyright.com. Requests to the Publisher for permission should be addressed to the Permissions Department, John Wiley & Sons, Inc., 111 River Street, Hoboken, NJ 07030, (201) 748-6011, fax (201) 748-6008, or online at www.wiley.com/go/permissions.

Limit of Liability/Disclaimer of Warranty: While the publisher and the author have used their best efforts in preparing this book, they make no representations or warranties with respect to the accuracy or completeness of the contents of this book and specifically disclaim any implied warranties of merchantability or fitness for a particular purpose. No warranty may be created or extended by sales representatives or written sales materials. The advice and strategies contained herein may not be suitable for your situation. You should consult with a professional where appropriate. Neither the publisher nor the author shall be liable for any loss of profit or any other commercial damages, including but not limited to special, incidental, consequential, or other damages.

For general information on our other products and services or technical support, please contact our Customer Care Department within the United States at (800) 762-2974, outside the United States at (317) 572-3993 or fax (317) 572-4002.

Wiley also publishes its books in a variety of electronic formats. Some content that appears in print may not be available in electronic books. For more information about Wiley products, visit our web site at www.wiley.com.

Library of Congress Cataloging-in-Publication Data:

Peebles, R. Donahue, 1960–
    The Peebles path to real estate wealth : how to make money in any market / R. Donahue Peebles, with J.P. Faber.
       p.   cm.
    Includes index.
    ISBN 978-0-470-37280-7 (pbk.)
1. Real estate investment–United States.   I. Faber, J. P. (James Paris), 1954–   II. Title.
    HD255.P44   2008
    332.63'240973–dc22

                                                                                    2008012234

Printed in the United States of America.

10   9   8   7   6   5   4   3   2   1

Contents

The good news about real estate investing is that anyone
can do it. Having said that, you need to do your
homework to make a superior investment.

Figuring out the value of a piece of property—what it's
really worth—is both an analytic and creative process. It
is also fundamental to making a good investment.

If you want to buy property, or protect property that is
now threatened by skyrocketing mortgage payments,
don't discount the power of government programs.

The average person who goes to a bank for a mortgage
figures it's not negotiable. Wrong. Here are a few helpful
insights to help you negotiate with the man behind the curtain.

To understand the current situation you have to look back
at historic real estate cycles, in particular to the real estate
crisis of the early 1990s.

A big aspect of the current real estate crisis is that it's
indiscriminant. It's hurting every market in the country,
even places with solid fundamentals. And that's where to buy.

The Opportunity of Setbacks (Why I Wrote This Book)

I started my real estate career in my twenties, working as an appraiser of low- and middle-income housing for HUD in Washington, D.C. That was in the late 1970s, during one of the worst real estate crises to rock this country. Despite those troubled times, by the mid 1980s I was developing my first office building and on my way to becoming a multimillionaire. Later, when the real estate market again crashed in the early 1990s, I invested heavily. Today I have a net worth approaching $400 million.

I am writing this book at a time when the real estate market is once again down. Most people would call this a bad real estate market, with prices dropping. For me, it is a market full of opportunities.

When I started working in real estate during that down market of the late 1970s, interest rates were at 20 percent. Times were tough, but it meant lots of work for me as an appraiser. I spent the ensuing years developing my real estate valuation skills and developing local business and political relationships. By the mid 1980s I had evolved those skills and contacts sufficiently to lay the foundation of my wealth, developing my first high-rise. It was not until the early 1990s, however, that I began to build a true real estate fortune.

This was in the midst of the last great real estate crisis in America. During this time the real estate industry faced a severe credit crunch, right when values were declining due to oversupply; the credit crunch expedited and exaggerated that decline. These factors combined to create the largest transfer of wealth in our country's history, when the big Wall Street firms decided to take a look at distressed real estate. It was then that the first private equity or vulture funds were formed by some of the largest investment banking firms in the world. They saw great opportunity and had access to the capital to take advantage of the situation.

I also built my fortune through buying well in those difficult years. It was a time of great opportunity for buyers who had two things: access to money and a strong stomach. I had both. My real estate appraisal business had grown into a real estate tax appeal business, which provided me with excess cash flow to invest, and I possessed a great appetite for taking calculated risks. (The operative word here is "calculated"!)

Today we have a situation that is presenting almost as good a buying opportunity as the last real estate crisis, certainly on the residential side. Once again we are flooded with too many homes, with prices that rose to unsustainable heights. Compounding the problem are millions of overblown mortgages for houses no longer worth as much as their loans, or with monthly payments that are no longer affordable by their owners.

The resulting market correction is shredding prices nationwide. Foreclosures are up, and consequently even more discounts are moving through the system.

Will prices drop further? Perhaps. But now is not the time to panic. Now is the time to hold on if you can, because at the end of the day real estate is going to endure. History has proven this; within five years of the end of the 1990s crash, real estate values recovered to exceed their pre-crisis levels. And they will do so again. Now is the time to refinance. Now is the time to buy.

My best real estate investments have always been opportunistic, based on challenging market conditions. If you want to be successful in real estate, you have to look for the opportunities within the challenges. Challenging times create fortuitous circumstances, and they are brought forth by particular setbacks. What you must do is find these opportunities as they present themselves. You just have to ask yourself the questions I asked myself during the last real estate/housing crisis in Washington: Is the real estate market now dead forever? Are people going to stop buying forever?

Most people get excited about real estate when the prices are going up. That's when everyone is buying. My concept runs contrary to that: Buy when fewer people are buying and sell when fewer people are selling. Follow that rule, and you will make a lot of money. Chase the market, and sometimes you'll end up getting caught; just like in the game of musical chairs, the music always stops. You lose if you're one of the last people still dancing. It's much wiser to have your seat well before then.

This book is about understanding the down real estate market and how to invest in that market. It's for the small and/or entrepreneurial investors, and it's about how they can make money, prosper, and get rich during this time period. It's also about how to survive and prosper in the current mortgage crisis and credit crunch, including how to save your home.

More than anything else it's about how you should think about real estate and the tools you'll need to execute these ideas, with practical advice on everything from where to look for real estate data to how to craft the best deal once you've focused on a particular piece of property. You need these tools because if you want to make money in real estate, you need to know the nature of the business. You need to be educated—to know what an option is, or how an auction works or what the difference is between Sallie Mae and Freddie Mac. To be forewarned is to be forearmed.

I remember how, at the height of the real estate collapse of the early 1990s, I wished I had more money to invest, some access to real capital. Now that I do, I am moving into huge projects in Las Vegas, Washington, D.C., Miami, and San Francisco. But I only got to this place through a series of deals that started with a vacant site in an economically neglected neighborhood, then my own house, then a few small vacant commercial storefront buildings, then a couple of vacant office buildings, then a large vacant warehouse, and then a prime development site.

After that it was one opportunity after the next, and in each case it was a matter of unlocking value: a historic bank building on F Street in Washington that I bought through an RTC auction and later turned into a Marriott Hotel; the Shorecrest Hotel that I bought on Miami Beach when it was a flea trap in 1996 for $5 million; followed by the Royal Palm Hotel for $5.5 million— buildings today that would be worth $80 million; the Bath Club, also on Miami Beach, which I bought in 1998 and then quadrupled in value overnight by getting it rezoned for a luxury high-rise condominium, that would be worth $120 million today; plus an 80-acre oceanfront site that I bought in Pacifica, south of San Francisco, for one-tenth its actual value because the owners were faced with a looming threat of having to pay for environmental reclamation (a former rock quarry, now to become an oceanfront resort). Our most recent purchases are in Las Vegas, 19.3 prime acres in the gaming/ resort district for $110 million that are now worth $338 million.

These deals are the subject of my other book, *The Peebles Principles*, which goes over them in detail. For our purposes here, I mention them mostly to illustrate that this book is not based on abstract principles, but on real markets and real transactions.

The other reason I mention them is that all of these deals were based on setbacks or depressed market conditions or the false perception of a depressed market, including the fundamental setback of buying in a down market—and that by overcoming those setbacks I created value. That is the really important message of this book. While I made my fortune buying in down real estate markets—an opportunity that has arrived once again—I really made my fortune by paying a low price in a challenging situation. And those opportunities will always present themselves, in any market.

Remember, your first investments don't have to be mega deals to be successful. One of my most lucrative investments was the condominium apartment I bought for my mother in 1991. At the time the market was dead, and I paid $125,000 for the property. Today it is worth $750,000. May all your deals turn out as well.

PART ONE

A RECENT HISTORY OF THE REAL ESTATE ROLLER COASTER

CHAPTER 1

The Big Bang: The Post-2000 Real Estate Explosion

*Between 2000 and 2006, mortgage interest rates in the
United States fell in half. That started a feeding frenzy,
which sent housing prices to dizzying heights.*

An investment bubble is just what it sounds like: a pocket of air, rising upwards until it bursts. In real estate, just as in other financial arenas, bubbles occur when demand for a product pushes its price well above what is rational. A kind of investment fever sets in, with one buyer selling to the next, until the final fool has paid the final inflated price: the time when the music stops and someone is left standing without a chair.

When the bubble pops, people can never quite believe they bought into the mass hysteria that drove prices so high. They come

3

to their senses, as if waking up from a collective dream. They remember saying to themselves: *It can't be this easy to make money.* But they ignored those thoughts and kept going. Well, they were correct. It's not that easy.

The great real estate bubble that rose between 2000 and 2006 was not the first of its kind. History is littered with the wreckage of past buying stampedes. From today's vantage point, many seem ludicrous, if not downright frightening. Even a cursory student of history is aware that the Great Depression followed that enormous bubble known as the Roaring Twenties, capped off by Black Tuesday and the collapse of the wildly overblown U.S. stock market.

Perhaps the most bizarre bubble in history was the tulip bulb craze of Holland, from 1634 to 1637. In retrospect, it is astonishing. At its peak, when the price of already expensive tulip bulbs rose 2,000 percent in one month, Dutch citizens were willing to trade their life savings, their land, even their homes for a handful of these unborn flowers.

Real estate bubbles do not seem quite as perverse, if only because at the end of the day you are still at least holding onto tangible property. And their causes seem more logical. The Florida real estate frenzy of the 1920s, for example, was predicated on a thriving U.S. economy combined with Florida's burgeoning popularity for people who were sick of being cold. The state's population was growing rapidly, and housing could not keep pace. By the mid 1920s, houses were quadrupling in value in less than a year. Condolike properties were going for more than $4,000,000 in 1925. And these are not adjusted prices!

The U.S. real estate bubble of the 2000s bears remarkable similarity to the Florida land boom of the 1920s. Back then, credit was easy to find, and people took on huge mortgages. Houses were trading hands like poker chips, and everybody was jumping in, even people with little money. Big capital was poured in as well, developing large residential tracts, golf course communities, retirement villages, and so forth. In one unique barometer of the boom, the *Miami Herald* was so jammed with real estate ads that in 1922 it became the heaviest newspaper in the world.

In the case of the great real estate bubble of the 2000s, the trigger was the availability of credit. The prime rate for the majority of top U.S.-chartered commercial banks, which had hovered at 8 percent or better for the last half of the 1990s, hit 9.5 percent in 2000. The rate then swiftly declined, sliding from 9.5 percent on Jan. 1, 2001 to 4.75 percent on Jan. 1, 2002. By mid-2003 the rate had bottomed out at 4 percent.

This fall in the prime rate—the interest rate charged by banks to their most creditworthy customers, including mortgagees—was the result of a parallel drop in rates by the Federal Reserve. This rate, officially the Federal Funds Target Rate, is the short-term, overnight rate at which banks can borrow money from the Federal Reserve. Its fall was even steeper, tumbling from 6.5 percent on January 1, 2001, to 1.75 percent on January 1, 2002, bottoming out in mid-2003 at 1 percent (see Figure 1.1).

The Federal Reserve lowered its interest rates partly in reaction to the dot-com bust and the consequent economic slowdown at the end of the roaring 1990s, a bust many believed was caused by too much tightening of Fed rates in the final years of that decade. The Fed wanted to restimulate the economy, and it did. Its 1 percent rate from mid-2003 to mid-2004 opened the door to massive liquidity in the marketplace. The rate climbed back to just over 5 percent by 2006, but by then the cat had been let out of the bag.

The cat, in this case, was a huge increase in purchasing power for home buyers, and it unleashed a buying fever that sent home sales soaring. And what a fever it was.

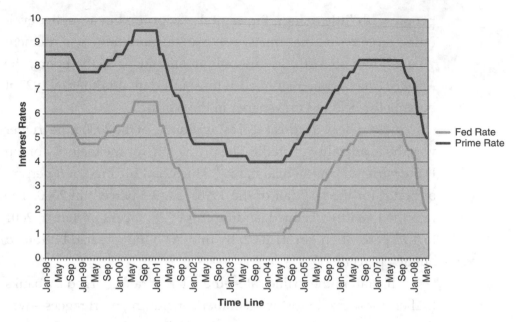

Figure 1.1   **Fed and Prime Rates, 1998–2008**

Source: Federal Reserve

Sales of new homes in the United States had remained fairly steady for decades prior to 2000, rising gradually as the twentieth century came to a close. In 1965 a total of 575,000 new homes were sold in the United States; ten years later the number was similar, at 549,000 new homes sold. By 1985, annual new home sales had inched up to 688,000, staying at that level for more than a decade; in 1995 the total was 667,000, for example.

But when the prime rate dropped and people could borrow money at much lower rates, all hell broke loose. In 2002, the number of new homes sold in the United States reached 908,000; by 2005, at the peak of the real estate boom, 1,283,000 new homes were sold. In other words, after increasing less than 20 percent over the three decades from 1965 to 1995, annual sales of new homes then doubled by 2005.

A similar rise took place in new home prices. While the average new home in the United States cost about $100,000 in 1985, and climbed to about $158,000 in 1995, by 2005 the average price of a new house came in at just under $300,000. By 2006, with the momentum still rolling, the average price had reached $305,000.

The median price for single-family homes in the United States—the combined price for new and previously owned homes—also rose at a good clip. Between April 2000 and April 2005, the median U.S. home price rose 55 percent to $206,000 (it would cross $230,000 in 2006). (See Figure 1.2.) Key urban markets climbed much faster, at blistering paces: up 135 percent in Los Angeles, 132 percent in San Diego, 117 percent in Las Vegas, 128 percent in Miami, and so on (see Figure 1.3).

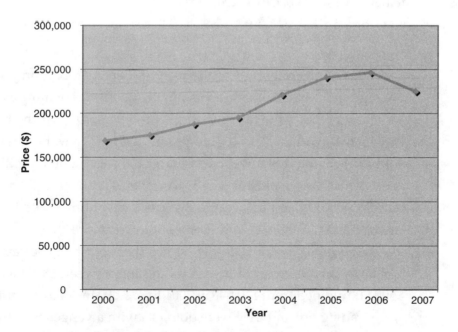

Figure 1.2   **Median Price of U.S. Homes, 2000–2007**

Source: U.S. Department of Housing and Urban Development

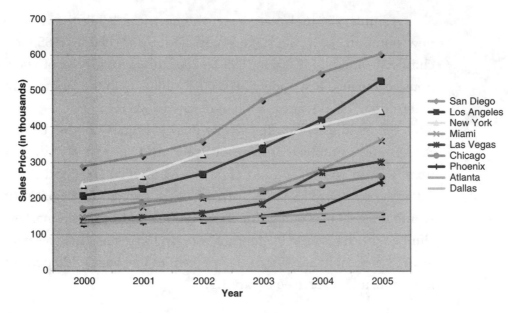

Figure 1.3   **Median Prices in U.S. Cities, 2000–2005**

Source: National Association of Realtors; S&P/Case-Shiller® Index

This paints only part of the picture, however. Not only were average and median prices rising, but the quantities of more expensive new homes were also soaring. At the beginning of the house buying frenzy, in the year 2001 for example, 75,000 new homes were sold in the United States for less than $100,000, while only 25,000 new homes were sold for more than $500,000. By 2005 the ratio had flipped. In that peak year, only 33,000 new homes sold for less than $100,000, while 144,000 homes sold for more than $500,000. The quantity of midpriced new homes that sold had escalated as well: The total number of homes selling for between $300,000 and $500,000 jumped from 110,000 in 2001 to 315,000 in 2005. Americans were trading up, and they were doing so with a vengeance.

There were other indicators, too, of how Americans took advantage of the lower interest rates to fuel their new buying mania.

Back in 1988, when the U.S. Census Bureau first started keeping comprehensive records of such things, 676,000 new homes were purchased. Of those, 62,000 were paid for with cash, 44,000 with Veteran Administration guarantees and 127,000 with FHA-insured loans—the rest were purchased using so-called conventional mortgages, larger loans that were not government insured.

By 2006, a year when more than a million new homes were purchased, the breakdown of how they were financed had radically changed. Only 38,000 were purchased with cash, 25,000 with VA guarantees, and 38,000 with FHA backing. All the rest—more than twice the number in 1988—were acquired using conventional mortgages, a sign of just how much liquidity had entered the system by virtue of lower lending rates. (See Figure 1.4.)

Of course, these so-called conventional mortgages were becoming more and more unconventional. In fact, many were being made at rates that were below the prime rate—to be subsequently increased or "adjusted"—which gave buyers even more power when it came to buying their dream homes.

A lot has been written about the so-called subprime mortgages—those made to borrowers with less than illustrious credit histories—and how they have been the leading edge of the mortgage meltdown. While that is partially correct, the real problem was not so much the fact that these were subprime mortgages but the fact that they were adjustable-rate mortgages, or ARMs. If people had simply gotten a fixed-rate mortgage, at a price they could afford, then the great mortgage meltdown of 2007–2008 might have been little more than an annoying market correction to the exorbitant cost of housing.

Instead, what happened was that greed took over and clouded the judgment of both buyers and those issuing the mortgages. What happened was that lenders offered better rates to homebuyers for

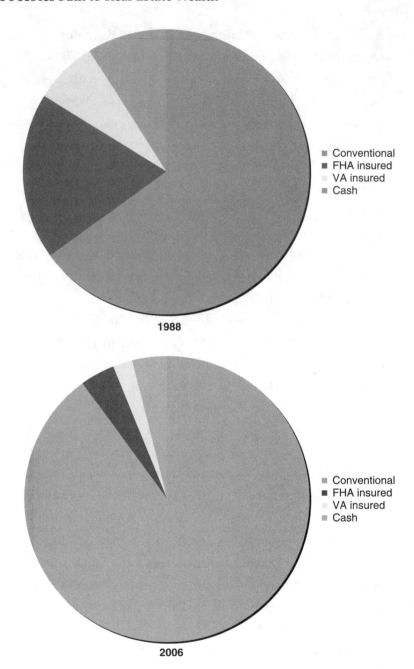

Figure 1.4   **New Home Financing, 1988 vs. 2006**

Source: U.S. Bureau of the Census

a period of time—two or three years—after which time the rates would rise. It was a great sales tool, like any upfront discounting, and buyers loved it. The consequence was a sudden surge in buying power.

Let's say someone who bought a home in the 1990s—1995, 1996, or 1997—was paying for a $500,000 mortgage. That mortgage had a fixed interest rate of 8 or maybe 9 percent. So the homeowner was paying $45,000 a year to service the debt. When interest rates went down, in 2001, 2002 and 2003, that same homeowner could borrow at between 4 and 5 percent with an adjustable-rate mortgage. All of a sudden, the same annual expense of $45,000 could buy a much larger, million-dollar home.

People looked at the options and couldn't resist. Most figured they could get twice the house for the same payment, and that is a powerful lure. The general consensus, as well, was that interest rates wouldn't go up anytime soon. Even if they did, homebuyers could lock in their adjustable mortgage rates for a couple of years. Most thought that by the time their adjustable rates rose, one of two things would have happened: They'd be making more money themselves, so they could afford the hike, or their homes would be worth more, so they could either refinance yet again or sell and take a profit.

Add to that mix the people who went even further out on the limb with exotic mortgages. Forget about simply paying low, later-to-be-adjusted rates. New lenders were out in the marketplace—companies like Countrywide Financial Corporation—and they, unlike banks, were willing to be far more lenient about down payments and finance 85, 90, 95, or even 100 percent of the value of a home. In many cases they didn't require payment on principal, only interest, at least for a stipulated number of years. They were even giving negative-amortization loans, where not only did the borrowers not pay principal; they didn't pay the full amount of interest either. They paid some part of the interest, and the rest of it was added to the principal.

Finally, you also had the psychological impact of low-cost mortgages on people who didn't have good credit, but who now were given an opportunity to buy homes for the first time. The lower interest rates brought hundreds of thousands, if not millions, of these new homebuyers into the market. And it was not just the lower rates; it was the nature of the lenders.

What you now had were aggressive mortgage companies that did not have the same criterion as banks, with little concern about whether you could repay the loan, and no concern for the communities where they were lending. They were too busy repackaging these loans with investment bankers on Wall Street and selling them off. They just wanted to make more loans and collect more fees. And as the newly available loans released more demand, prices rose. It seemed, in fact, as though they would continue rising forever; new buyers wanted to get in on the action before their long-cherished dream of homeownership escaped them once again.

The result was that overall U.S. homeownership grew from 64 percent in 1994—where it had been for more than a decade—to more than 69 percent in 2004, its all-time peak.

To cap it all off, you had people who neither bought nor sold, but simply refinanced and cashed in on the value of their homes as prices continued to rise. In fact, an estimated 34 million households took money out of their homes 2003–2007, roughly one-third of the nation. And why not? Let's say you lived in San Francisco. Between June 2000 and June 2004, the average price of a home in San Francisco increased by almost 45 percent. If you owned a house that was worth $400,000 in the summer of 2000, by the summer of 2004 it would have been worth $580,000.

Now, to continue our example, suppose you started out with a mortgage for $350,000 at 8 percent. That's a monthly interest payment of $2,333 (let's forget about principal for the moment). Suddenly, with an adjustable mortgage at 4.5 percent, you could free up $180,000 in cash and pay less—about $1,988 a month—for your interest payments. Who cares if your monthly payments would rise to $2,870 a month two years later, and then climb from there. You'd be making more money by then, or your house would be worth even more, so you could refinance it again if need be.

All of this worked just fine in the context of the real estate bubble. As long as housing prices continued to rise, then these risky, exotic mortgages would be able to cover themselves. And everyone bought into it, including the investment bankers on Wall Street who packaged up these risky loans and sold them as investments—and, of course, those investors who acquired them.

The most aggressively discounted of the adjustable rate mortgages were offered to people with great credit. I myself was offered a loan at 3 percent for my house in Coral Gables, Florida, with some negative amortization included. I could have borrowed $10 million. In the end I borrowed three and a half million on a home that was worth $12 million; I got a 4 percent adjustable rate mortgage fixed for five years. That way I didn't have to deal with it for quite some time, and after the five-year period the rate could rise only 1 percent a year. I figured by then I'd refinance it or pay it off with cash, plus I never planned on being there for 30 years. The important thing was that I was able to borrow almost two million dollars more while my monthly payment went up only about $1,000. Just think about that. It's unbelievable.

So these exotic types of mortgages, these creative mortgages, were available to people with good credit. And those people with good credit said it was high time to use that good credit to leverage real estate, to get more house for the money, or to start using that credit to release money to invest in other things. Billions and billions of dollars in real estate assets were made liquid, and that capital chased higher-priced housing, which of course drove values even higher.

The American public was mesmerized by the bubble—and not just for their own, primary homes. Next came second homes and vacation properties, and then properties that investors bought on spec, especially condos. As each new price barrier was broken, more investors wanted in on the act. In condo-crazed Miami–Dade County, for example, some 100,000 new condo units were on the drawing board at the height of the bubble—in a county with 829,000 households.

In the end less than half of the units planned for Miami–Dade County will ever be finished. And just as in the great Dutch tulip

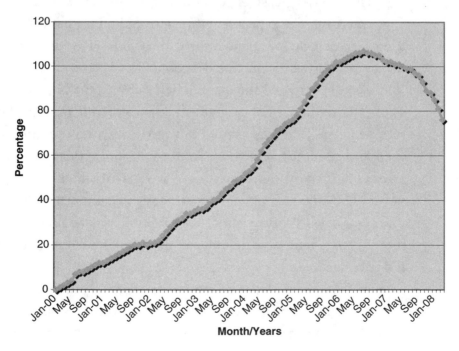

Figure 1.5   **Average U.S. Housing Prices, 2000–2008**
Source: S&P/Case-Shiller® Index

craze, the last investor caught in the cycle as it peaked will pay the price—at least the price of the down payment for that speculative condominium.

The problem with bubbles is that they are just so hypnotic; if you are not part of the action you tend to panic, to feel that if you don't jump in now you will miss out on the opportunity. In the case of U.S. housing, the bubble continued to rise year after year. According to the S&P/Case-Shiller U.S. National Home Price Index, the average price of a home in the largest 20 metropolitan markets in this country more than doubled between January 2000 and January 2006. In the hottest markets, the prices rose even faster. That kind of a bubble is hard to ignore. (See Figure 1.5.)

What you will learn in the rest of this book, however, is that if you want to make a lot of money in real estate, you must resist the herd mentality that takes place during a bubble. In order to do that you must fully understand the phenomenon and its fallout. So next we take a look at the environment that the great real estate bubble of the 2000s left in its wake: oversupply.

CHAPTER 2

The Great Flood: The Oversupply of Housing

Combined with the growing thirst for inventory, spiraling prices encouraged developers to build more projects. And guess what? Blind to the downturn, they built way too much.

For me, the sign that the real estate market was really out of control at its peak in 2005 and 2006 was when nightclub owners and nightclub promoters in Miami and Las Vegas were getting into the high-rise development business, calling themselves developers and actually getting financing for their projects. Granted, real estate is not an overly complicated business, but the high-rise construction business is; I guess the club promoters and the banks underwriting them had never heard the old saying "crawl before you walk." In this case it wasn't even a matter of walking. These people, who had never even been on the track, were now running in the Olympics.

The reality is that it does take some experience and a track record to know what to expect at the higher levels. Nonetheless, here you had amateurs who hadn't previously built anything, throwing up major high-rises in major world markets. Suddenly everybody was in the business of developing, and they were flooding their markets with more product than the consumers could absorb; like a rainstorm in a desert, the storm of unrestrained building created a dangerous flash flood of oversupply.

Another sign that the market was careening toward disaster was the way the latest crop of developments promoted themselves. Because there were so many projects out there, it got to the point where only the slickest advertising campaigns could compete. Forget the nicest kitchens or the best locations with the best views; you had to spend more money on advertising, have sexier models posing in those ads, offer more incentives to the brokers, and be more lavish with the parties that launched your project.

It was a real epiphany in mid-2005 when the *New York Times* ran a front page story about Miami's condo-launch party circuit, with a picture of a flavored oxygen bar at one of the presale events. The article was entitled "Salsa Dancers and Stunt Men? Must Be a Miami Condo Project." How different the title of an article on the front page of the *Times* business section at the end of 2007—"Condos, Condos, Everywhere"—discussing Miami's condo bloat and how the city's top condo developer Jorge Perez was being sued by dozens of disgruntled customers.

Indeed, Miami is now faced with the hangover from all that real estate revelry, namely an oversupply of product that was predicted to take the city, as of 1st Q 2008, an estimated 29 months to absorb. While Miami is the poster boy of real estate excess, it is by no means alone in the housing glut. Also as of 1st Q 2008, Detroit had a

19-month housing backlog, Las Vegas a 17-month supply, Tampa a 16-month supply, and Phoenix a 12-month supply. A healthy market should have 6 months or less.

So how did all this overbuilding take place?

Remember how interest rates for borrowers fell like a stone at the end of 2001, unleashing the first waves of new homebuyers? That same low-interest credit was not just limited to consumers. It was also extended to developers—the major commercial developers and the major national home construction companies—as well as to individual entrepreneurs of all stripes.

All of a sudden there was an enormous amount of money out there, combined with a sharp spike in demand not only from the average American homebuyer, whose buying power was now exponentially multiplied, but also from the luxury vacation homebuyer and the condo speculator. The result was that the same sort of fever that gripped homebuyers also gripped homebuilders. All across the United States, especially in California, Florida, and the hot Southwest Sunbelt markets, home construction companies expanded to meet the new demand.

To understand why homebuilders went overboard, all you have to do is appreciate the enormity of the demand. Not only did low interest rates significantly expand the buying power of existing homeowners, it also brought hordes of new homebuyers into the market. In many instances, after taxes were taken into consideration, it became less expensive to own than it was to rent. Everyone who was renting could now jump into the real estate game. In many cases renters were, in fact, encouraged to do so by developers who were buying their buildings and converting them into condominiums. The people who were renting the apartments then bought them as condos. As more apartment buildings were converted, the supply of rental property started shrinking, encouraging more home ownership.

The market had also just come off something of a slow spell, which combined the last vestiges of the real estate collapse of the early 1990s with the sagging economy of the new millennium, the famed dot.com implosion and the consequent stock market decline from 2000 to 2002. So there wasn't a lot of demand at the turn of the century, and therefore not a lot of housing inventory on hand.

You then had a burst of thirst for inventory, and not enough inventory out there to slake that thirst. The market responded by creating more product, in this case more developments, more projects, more homes. Everyone tried to catch up with the demand and take advantage of it. You had new homebuyers entering the market, and you had people trading up. The new homebuyers were willing to pay premium prices for homes that were already owned, and the people selling them were stepping up to new—and bigger—residences.

Altogether it created a classic seller's market, one of the strongest in decades, with more buyers than sellers. Just about any product could be put on the market and sell quickly. My cousin, when she and her family moved down from Washington, D.C., to Florida to work for me in 2004, put their house on the market and within two days had people bidding more than the listed price. It wasn't just their house; people all across the country were bidding above list price for $500,000, $600,000, and $700,000 homes. Prices spiked. The median price of a house in the United States was pushed from $177,000 in February 2001 to $276,000 in June of 2006. House prices in many cities more than doubled.

With so much demand and prices rising so swiftly, home-builders rose to meet the challenge. Predictably, they flooded the market. How big was the flood? According to the federal government, at the end of 2000, there was an inventory of 301,000 new homes for sale in the United States. By the end of 2006, when interest rates had already returned to their early 2001 levels, there were 537,000 new homes for sale.

The supply of U.S. housing—or oversupply, in this case—can also be gauged by the number of new housing starts in the country. In 1995, there were 1.35 million new housing starts nationwide; in 2000 there were 1.57 million new housing starts; in 2005, there were 2.07 million housing starts. (By 2007, when the party was over, the number of housing starts was back down to the 1995 number of 1.35 million. By then, the seller's market had turned into a buyer's market.) (See Figures 2.1 through 2.3.)

The homebuilding firms themselves were on a growth binge, and the bigger ones just got bigger. In 2000, the top 10 homebuilders controlled about 10 percent of the U.S. market. By 2005 that share had reached 25 percent. D. R. Horton, for example, bought Schuler Homes, Inc., in 2002 for $653 million, an acquisition that raised

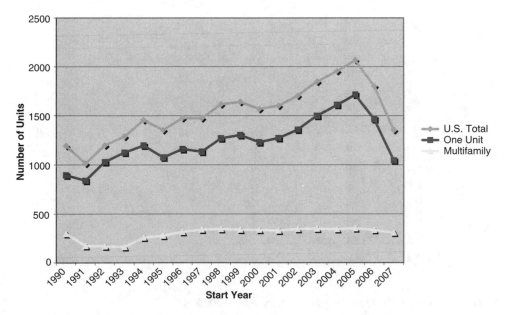

Figure 2.1   **U.S. Housing Starts, 1990–2007**

Source: U.S. Bureau of the Census

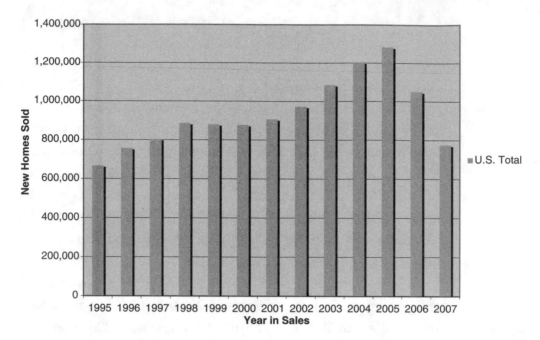

Figure 2.2   **New Home Sales 1995–2007**

Source: U.S. Bureau of the Census; HUD

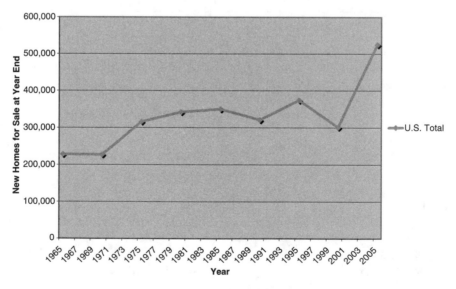

Figure 2.3   **New U.S. Housing Inventory, 1965–2005**

Source: U.S. Department of Housing and Urban Development

their profile overnight. The CEOs of the homebuilding companies began acting like rock stars, and bringing in the salaries of investment bankers. In 2004, the CEO of KB Homes took home $23.9 million, the CEO of Centex $19 million, and the CEO of Horton $8.7 million.

In retrospect it is remarkable how blind the builders were to the coming tsunami and how they themselves would drown in the oversupply. How out of touch were the builders? At the end 2005 D.R. Horton, the largest U.S. homebuilder in terms of unit volume, predicted that any downturn would be short-lived, and that they would sell 100,000 homes a year by 2010, almost double the 51,172 they sold in fiscal 2005. Pulte, the Number Two homebuilder in terms of unit sales, that same year forecast earnings growth of 20 to 25 percent for 2006, 2007, and 2008.

The pundits, too, were less than lucid about the situation. With prices starting to slip in the third quarter of 2006, Donald L. Kohn, vice chairman of the Fed, told the Atlanta Rotary Club in January 2007 that the worst would soon be over and that in his judgment "housing starts may be not very far from their trough." Even as things got worse in 2007, industry professionals were hopeful for an upturn in 2008. The National Association of Realtors predicted in May 2007 that existing home sales would reach 6.29 million in 2007, down from 6.48 million in 2006, but just a dip on their way back to those 2006 numbers in 2008. They also predicted 864,000 new home sales in 2007, down from 1.05 million in 2006, but on their way to back up to 936,000 in 2008. (See Figure 2.5.)

The actual numbers for 2007 were 5.6 million in sales of existing homes (almost 700,000 less than forecast) and 774,000 in sales of new homes (closer, but still 90,000 off the mark). Needless to say, their predictions for 2008 are now less rosy. (See Figure 2.4.)

There were other ramifications to this red-hot builders' market as well. Developers were so intent on meeting demand that they

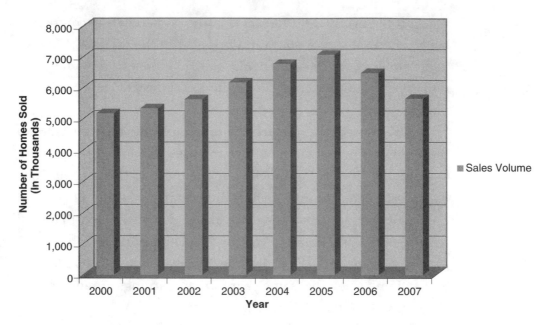

Figure 2.4   **Sales of Existing Homes, 2000–2007**

Source: National Association of Realtors

began converting commercial buildings to condominiums in places like San Francisco, Chicago, and other parts of the country. Office sites, new hotel sites, former hotels—developers were converting all of them to residential. What that did was to significantly shrink the supply of hotels and office buildings. In San Francisco, for example, you went in a couple of years from class-A office rental rates of $35 to $40 a foot to $75 to $80 a foot. I have to say that amidst all the debris of the mortgage crisis this side effect was one of the most interesting. Those investors who went against the residential tide, and who developed commercial properties instead, in the end made a killing. Those investors who bought commercial properties did the same.

The overbuilding also impacted construction costs. There was such a rush to put product on the market that the price to build was driven up. After all, there was only so much material available. The pace of manufacturing at plants that churned out building materials and supplies was based on the normal pace of the marketplace, a multi-decade rhythm that suddenly got kicked up a notch. On a global basis, there were also concrete and steel shortages, thanks to huge new demand from China.

Not only couldn't you get materials quickly enough; there weren't enough people to do the work. The labor pool couldn't meet the demand of construction. So what happened? The cost of building went up significantly. In one year alone—between 2003 and 2004—construction costs in South Florida went up 25 percent.

Naturally, this poured fuel onto the pricing fire. Not only did demand push prices higher, construction expenses added their own pressure to the cost of an average house or condominium. You couldn't build a house or condo for the same money anymore. (Ironically enough, this only encouraged the larger homebuilders, because they had the benefit of economies of scale and the clout to buy existing supplies.)

It was a great market if you owned property. Conversely, it was harder to make money if you were a buyer, unless you bought and sold quickly; you have to catch a rising market before it peaks, or you get caught holding the bag. And it did peak—the music stopped somewhere in 2006—and everyone with property for sale in that market got caught. In the end, as with all drunken sprees, the participants were faced with a morning after.

This was certainly true for the big homebuilders, who started losing money toward the end of 2006. First, they were hit by falling land prices. In Florida, for example, residential land prices that had climbed tenfold from 2000 to 2005 abruptly receded 50 percent by the end of 2006. Similar drops occurred in other states, and the top five U.S. homebuilders—D.R. Horton, Pulte Homes, Lennar, Centex, and Toll Brothers—collectively lost $1.47 billion in land value in the last quarter of 2006. Pulte alone wrote off $350 million for land in the fourth quarter of 2006.

The following year was worse. In 2007, when the bottom started falling out of housing prices, the top U.S. homebuilders would collective lose nearly $20 billion. Lennar alone lost $1.9 billion in 2007, and by the first quarter of 2008, 13 sizable U.S. home-builders (though none of the better financed and more diversified top 5) would declare bankruptcy.

Now, part of the reason these companies—the ones that flooded the market with new supply—couldn't put the brakes on sooner was because they had so much product in the pipeline. Reversing the momentum was like trying to change the direction of an ocean liner; there was just no way to turn on a dime.

But why was there so much in the pipeline? To answer that, you have to look at how lending practices in the industry had changed over the years.

Since the 1960s, annual new home sales remained relatively constant in the United States. From 1965 to 1995, the figures oscillated between 500,000 and 700,000, and not always in an upward direction. In 1975, for example, 549,000 new homes were sold, 15,000 more than were sold in 1995.

During that time, however, the number of new homes that were sold prior to construction jumped significantly. In 1975, for example, just 84,000 of new home sales were for houses not-yet-started. By 1995 (when fewer homes were sold) the number of not-yet-started homes that sold had climbed to 205,000. By 2005, the height of the recent housing boom, the number of presold homes had more than doubled again, to 503,000.

Why were so many homes presold? This was largely a consequence of the way in which banks were making commercial loans.

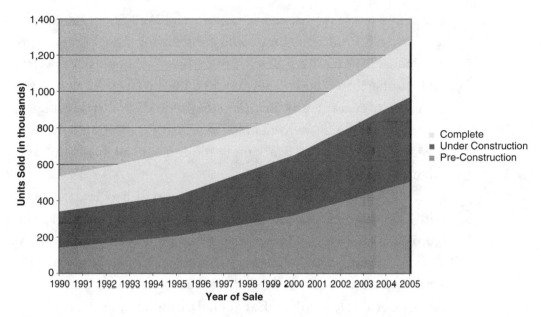

Figure 2.5   **New Home Sales, Pre-Construction vs. Built, 2000–2005**

Source: National Association of Home Builders

The principal qualification for receiving commercial loans from banks on big development projects from the 1990s onward was the presale. If you had a sufficient amount of presold units, banks would lend you the necessary funds for construction. Not only that, banks would lend you much higher percentages of the construction costs, so long as they had assurances of presales. It got to the point where developers could borrow 90 percent, even 95 percent of a project cost—and we are talking hundreds of millions of dollars here, with no recourse, which means no personal obligations—so long as there were enough presales. No wonder condo developers spent so lavishly on their launch parties!

And guess who started making more and more of these pre-construction loans? Not the conservative, mainstream banks, but the Wall Street investment banks, selling these loans to the secondary market as mortgage-backed securities. The Wall Street banks had less stringent criteria, so they could compete for these big commercial loans. Standard, regulated banks, like The Bank of America, had tougher loan criteria. They required the developer or the parent company to guarantee the loan, and they wouldn't allow leveraging of more than 75 or 80 percent of the loan. So they lost out to the new breed of lenders; there was simply too much available credit and too many entities making loans.

I myself will never forget a conversation I had in early 2007 with a banking executive friend of mine at Bank of America. He was telling me how quiet it was, because he couldn't make any loans. They were doing $30 million loans, but they couldn't compete with Wall Street firms on the $100 million-plus loans, because they were being offered at lower than the national prime lending rate and with no recourse. It was the same thing that happened with mortgages. Countrywide, which was not a national bank or a savings bank, became the nation's top mortgage lender.

Which brings us back to the final part of the puzzle, the presales. The lenders created the situation with their requirements for presales, but where was the demand coming from?

The answer is not as simple as saying "from homebuyers." Because what you are talking about here is a home that you cannot move into right away, one that you will have to wait two or more years to occupy. The people who buy these sorts of units are typically second-home buyers looking for a good deal. Or investors, a.k.a. speculators.

I think the overall concept of speculating on residential real estate is generally a mistake. Residential real estate is not an investment—well, it is—but for most people it's not as much a monetary investment as it is an investment in lifestyle. The good news about this investment in lifestyle is that it can make money for you; you build up equity by paying down your debt, and the real estate values keep pace with inflation while you're living in it. That is the fundamental rubric of residential real estate.

I think the condo craze, and the prepaid housing project craze, really created this environment of investor mentality. Because who is going to buy a one- or two-bedroom home that's only going to be delivered in three years? Normally, people who make those kinds of purchases are in some sort of transition. It's either their first home purchase, and they need that preconstruction discount, or it's on the flip side, empty nesters who are not in that much of a rush to move into their final retirement residence but want it custom made.

Now came a new type of residential buyer, the individual speculator whose goal was to buy and flip until, as in our proverbial game of musical chairs, there was no one left to flip to. According to the National Association of Realtors, by the first half of 2005 about 18 percent of all new and existing homes were being purchased by investors or second-home owners. By 2006 as many as 40 percent of housing customers in the urban markets were speculators, especially condominium buyers. In some new condo complexes in suburban Washington and downtown Miami, virtually every buyer was a speculator.

Regardless of the causes, however—whether it was the plethora of speculators or the overexuberance of homebuilders—the result was the same: a substantial oversupply of housing. Nonetheless, because so much of the new housing was presold, the construction loans were made and developers were still contractually obligated to deliver on their projects.

This would have been a problem under any circumstance, but you had another double whammy. Thanks to more supply than demand, prices were starting to fall, but the higher costs for construction and materials were still holding constant. Why? Forget the burgeoning international hunger for raw materials; the contractors were not only working away on residential projects still in the pipeline, they were also busy trying to satisfy the renewed demand from the neglected office and hospitality markets.

The result was a fierce dilemma for homebuilders. It was no longer economic to build new product—you couldn't sell it for more than it cost, or even at cost in some cases—but thousands of units were under contract. This was true for everyone from the single high-rise developer to massive homebuilders like Lennar or Pulte. They all began to suffer radically; even the Wall Street investors who brought much of the problem on themselves recognized this, hammering down the overall stock values of homebuilders by two-thirds in 2006 and 2007.

One of the first national name brands to actually collapse was Levitt & Sons, a unit of the famed Levitt Corporation, the company that practically invented the modern suburb after World War II. Having pioneered the concept of the planned community with its Levittown in Long Island—along with other similar suburban spreads in New Jersey and Pennsylvania—it was no great leap for Levitt & Sons to use its good name with the very baby boomer generation that had been born and raised in its suburban visions six decades earlier.

What Levitt & Sons did was to push the concept of retirement communities, with new homes clustered around recreation centers that came with tennis and bocce courts, fitness gyms, indoor and outdoor pools, even ballrooms, card rooms, and billiard rooms. Unfortunately, they too were swept up by the times, and overextended themselves into 18 such communities, many of them in Florida. By late 2007, with way too much product and way too little demand, they ran out of money and declared bankruptcy. Today the various pieces of its retirement community empire are being sorted out and sold off.

Interestingly enough, that fabled brand, which made its name by providing entry-level housing for young couples, had also been sucked into the upgrade hysteria. The original homes in the 1950s, which cost about $7,000, would have been priced at less than $100,000 in today's equivalent dollars. Instead, the new Levittown homes, with made-to-order granite-topped kitchens and whirlpool bathrooms, were priced all the way up to $450,000.

Those units won't be finding buyers at such prices any time soon. Most people who could afford to buy luxury homes, and wanted to, have bought them. For that matter, most people who wanted to buy a home, period, have done so. As a result we have an excess of homes nationwide, with more than a 12-month supply of inventory, 100 percent more than is healthy. We now need new people coming into the housing market or a shift in demographics.

Until that happens, we have what is known as a buyer's market.

CHAPTER 3

Down Time: The New Buyer's Market

*Because of the credit crunch and the oversupply,
we are now on the down slope of the housing bubble,
with prices dropping across the country. That means
opportunities are everywhere.*

We are now in the midst of a classic buyer's market.

What exactly does that mean? It means that the buyers have the upper hand. To put it another way, in the ebb and flow of supply and demand, there is now more supply than demand. And when that happens the value of what's being supplied tends to fall, as sellers lower their prices to attract buyers. This is basic, classic economics, the pure capitalism of the marketplace. If everyone wants an apple and there are only a few for sale, you can charge more. If there are lots of apples and not many takers, you have to charge less.

Another way to picture the real estate market: you have a manufacturer, who is the developer, and you have a wholesaler, who is the investor, and you have a consumer, who is the end user. The challenge is that we don't have enough consumers right now. With their ranks thinning, sales of new homes fell 26 percent in 2007; sales of existing single-family homes fell 13 percent. By March of 2008, new home sales were off 36 percent from March of the previous year, while existing-home sales were off 19.3 percent from the year earlier.

So in the current environment the buyer is king, especially in certain overbuilt cities. The result is the signature phenomenon of a buyer's market in real estate: the fall of property prices. And that's just what has happened. Since the real estate bubble started coming back to earth from its height in 2005–2006, average prices nation-wide have fallen by about 14.8 percent—at least as of February 2008, based on the S&P/Case-Shiller Index of 20 metropolitan areas.

In overheated markets like Las Vegas, Phoenix, San Deigo, Los Angeles, and Miami, where typical prices rose by more than 150 percent, the drop has been steeper. From the peak of the residential market—the month of July 2006, according to S&P/Case-Shiller—to February 2008, prices in Las Vegas fell 24.3 percent, in Phoenix 24 percent, in San Diego 23.6 percent, in Los Angeles 21.5 percent and in Miami 21.4 percent.. (See Figures 3.1 and 3.2.)

Another measure of demand, and hence value, is asking price: the price for which properties are listed, but not necessarily sold. Based on asking prices (compiled from Realtor MLS listings), the U.S. real estate market peaked in the summer of 2005. In Los Ange-les, the median asking price for a house in August of that year was

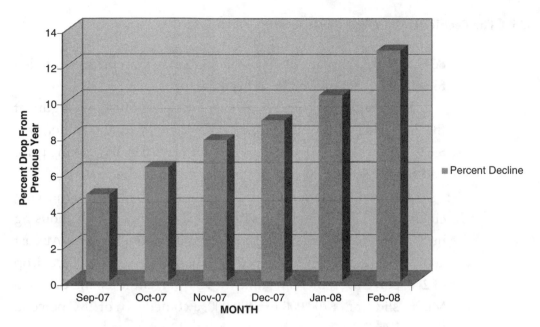

Figure 3.1 **Price Drops, 2007–2008**

Source: S&P/Case-Shiller® Index

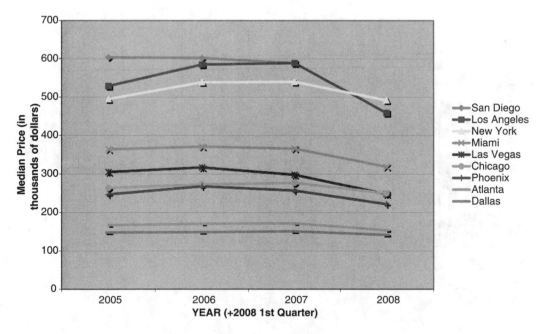

Figure 3.2 **Home Prices in U.S. Cities, 2005–2008**

Source: National Association of Realtors

$649,999. By February of 2008, the median asking price had fallen to $499,900, a 23 percent drop from the top.

High-end asking prices fell even more steeply. L.A.'s figure at the 75th percentile, or three-quarters of the way up the ladder, was $999,000 as of mid August 2005. By February 2008, that asking price had fallen to $725,000, a 27 percent retreat from the peak.

The same pattern holds true for most of the other high-flying cities around the United States that were big jumpers in the housing bubble. In Miami, for example, the median asking price in August 2005 was $425,000; by February 2008 it had fallen to $320,000, a drop of 24.7 percent. At the same time the 75th percentile asking prices in Miami slid from $700,000 to $499,000, a comedown of 28.7 percent. (See Figure 3.3.)

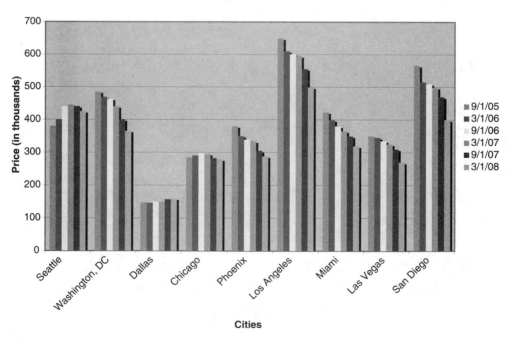

Figure 3.3   **Top City Asking Prices, 2005–2008**

Source: HousingTracker

As you might expect, the cities where prices have been falling the fastest are those where they went up the fastest during the housing bubble; cities with slower price gains are seeing less depreciation in the buyer's market. San Francisco's home prices climbed 117.6 percent from the beginning of June 2000 to their peak in July 2006; by February of 2008 they had receded 19.7 percent. Compare that to Boston, where prices rose a more modest 77.7 percent during the boom, but then fell just 9.8 percent on the early 2008 down slope.

Likewise, in the rare cases where prices have only started to come down in 2008, and then just slightly—most notably Seattle, Charlotte, and Portland, Oregon—prices also rose at modest rates during the housing bubble.

Also as you might expect, cities and regions where prices climbed at a moderate clip were less prone to an overabundance of new building during the boom. Among other factors, they were less attractive to retiring baby boomers, second-home buyers, and speculators in the first place. Not a lot of retirees chose Chicago over Phoenix as the place to spend their golden years, and not a lot of vacation-home buyers picked Portland over San Diego. But the hot markets became overbuilt, and now have an unhealthy backlog of properties, which pushes prices down and makes them a buyer's market.

Think of it this way. If you took all the new condos away from downtown Miami, how strong would that market be? The same goes for all the other markets with excess homebuilding. Think about how strong those markets would be if you removed the new inventory.

You can look at each market that way. Prices in Miami wouldn't be declining if it didn't have an inventory of 52,000 homes for sale in early 2008, where it had 12,000 for sale in 2005. Nor would Las Vegas, where 27,500 homes were for sale in 2008, compared to 16,000 in 2005. Nor would Washington, D.C., where 11,000 homes were for

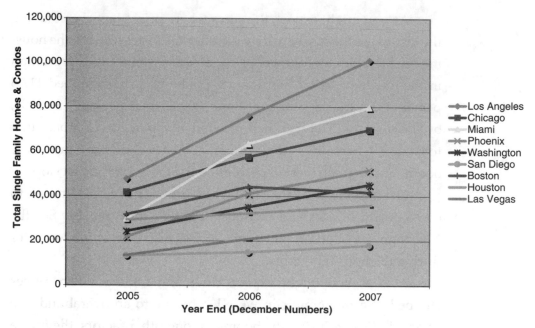

Figure 3.4   **Housing Inventory Overload**

Source: ZipRealty

sale in 2008, compared to 5,300 in 2005. It's all about the inventory, and it's the slow absorption of that inventory that's created the buyers market. (See Figure 3.4.)

On the flip side of the coin, and making matters worse for sellers, is a buying pool that's been constricted. Why? Because not only did interest rates go up (although the Fed has brought them back down in a panic), the mortgage crisis has created a tightening of underwriting criteria. Banks, rather than mortgage companies, will begin making more of the loans—and they are going to require better credit, appropriate income, and substantial down payments.

So now you have fewer buyers than you've had in years, coupled with more supply. The two combine to create a perfect storm for the seller—and a golden opportunity for the qualified buyer.

Another big reason that prices have been going down is because, to put it bluntly, the average home had simply become overvalued. Beyond the logical pressures of supply and demand, you had the madness of the bubble. People were acting irrationally, offering to pay more than houses were worth. How can anybody go out and buy a home when other people are paying more than the asking prices? I mean, you write a contract for the full asking price, and the broker comes back and tells you, um, they've already got three full-price offers, how much higher are you prepared to go? The market couldn't sustain that kind of inflation.

This is also why you should never buy in a rapidly rising market like the recent bubble. Remember, the way to create wealth in real estate is through buying value. But during the bubble there were no deals to be had, no bargains; someone else was always willing to pay more for the property you wanted to buy. You can't make money as a buyer in that kind of environment.

As a seller, however, you were in the catbird seat. You could take an average, nondescript home and it became a million dollar home. My father's house, which was located in suburban Washington, D.C., should never have sold for the $600,000 he got for it at the height of the boom. It just shouldn't have. It was an average house, less than 2,200 square feet. It was a cute average house and above the cut for the neighborhood, granted, but average houses should not command such premiums. Look at how little you got for a million dollars at the height of the boom in a market like Miami, or Washington, D.C., or San Francisco, or Los Angeles. Those homes were just overvalued.

That, however, is the nature of a bubble. Everyone falls under a hypnotic spell, and bases decisions as much on the perception of the marketplace as its reality.

Perception works in both directions, by the way. Once a downturn begins, even cities with good economic fundamentals, ones that hadn't gone wild in the boom, are affected by the national mood of being in a down cycle. The media enhances it , as when CNBC's *Mad Money* star Jim Cramer told the audience of the *Today Show* in 2007, "Don't you dare buy a home now, you will lose money." So you get even less demand.

That's what makes it a buyer's market, when the air suddenly rushes out of the bubble. In Atlanta, for example, a three-bedroom house that fetched $330,000 at the height of the boom was later auctioned off for $134,000 by the bank that foreclosed on it. Another Atlanta property that sold for $255,000 in the summer of 2004 sold for $78,000 at auction in 2007. And this is a city that, by and large, was not rocked by the bubble as much as other cities. Its housing price index rose only 35 percent during the boom years (compared to 115 percent for New York, for example), and its average price had only fallen 2.5 percent by early 2008.

Even in cities like Atlanta, though, which had good economic fundamentals—and still does—the boom and subsequent buyer's market have both been pushed as much by perception as by realities. Even in cities where the fundamentals are good, demand has so waned that you can find a buyer's market. That's when you start to see that real estate not only varies significantly from region to region, and from city to city, but from neighborhood to neighborhood.

Take Chicago, for example. The Windy City was not as blown away as much as others by the housing bubble; values there increased just 67.5 percent from January 2000 to July 2006 (Los Angeles jumped 174 percent, by comparison) and retreated only 3.5 percent by the end of 2007. But within the city, the pattern was not homogeneous. The average sale price for a home in the Lincoln Park neighborhood at the end of 2007, for example, was $480,000, down 17.6 percent from a year earlier. The average sale price for a home in the Lakeview neighborhood was $461,522, up 7.4 percent from the year before. A buyer's market is there, but not in every sector of the city.

All of this goes to say that, in the current mortgage crisis, there are many markets where the overall economic fundamentals are still strong, where the overbuilding wasn't atrocious, and where the undertow from the nationwide drop in housing prices is not justified. These may not be obvious buyer's markets, until you discern the shifts in specific neighborhoods and take advantage of national perceptions that are making sellers panic and buyers stay away.

On the other hand, there are obvious buyer's markets out there. A good example is the Cape Coral–Fort Myers metropolitan area in southwest Florida, once a hotbed of housing development and price escalation. In the first half-decade of the millennium, home prices in many cases tripled in value. With national homebuilders anxious to cash in, the ensuing building frenzy transformed the economy; by 2005 real estate and construction accounted for one in four jobs.

In 2007 the boom went bust. By midyear, the number of housing permits in the Fort Myers area had fallen by 70 percent from a year earlier, and by the end of the year, housing prices had already returned to their 2002 levels. By the middle of that year as well, unemployment had grown to a rate of 4.7 percent, almost double the 2.5 percent jobless rate in 2004. The local economy had grown by feeding on its own real estate frenzy, and when the bubble burst, the community did not have the fundamentals to justify such high-flying housing values.

A local economy that is well diversified, or at least not dependent on real estate as a major employer, should naturally enough not be subject to the same sort of real estate collapse. If prices in such markets fall as sharply as those in weak markets, then this is where buyers should look for opportunities. In a certain sense, these areas are even more of a buyer's market, since they will recover more rapidly.

Washington, D.C., for example, should be a good place to take advantage of the national oversupply impacting local prices. In D.C., just one job in eight was tied to the real estate and construction industry at the peak of the boom. And Washington, seat of the federal government, is a major employment center, which gives it a strong foundation for housing demand when the national market begins to return.

Compare that to poor Detroit, where housing prices only rose 23.24 percent during the boom, but have fallen 14.6 percent since, a decline second only to San Diego, where prices had enjoyed a 149 percent bump. Detroit, the auto capital of the United States, has terrible fundamentals at the present time. Although it's a buyer's market, it probably won't come back as soon as a city like Washington, D.C.

Even dreadfully overbuilt markets like Miami and Las Vegas have certain underlying market motivators that will eventually lead to a restoration in prices. Miami will still attract Latin Americans and Europeans, for instance, and in Las Vegas, where the population has been growing at a pace of 7,000 people per month, the tourism industry is still producing significant numbers of new jobs. Both still have good weather and no state income tax.

You will also be more likely to find wild deals in places like Miami, Las Vegas or San Diego, since these are the most likely places where people have second homes. Now that things have tightened up, and adjustable-rate mortgages have gone up, these owners may have trouble making both their primary- and second-home mortgage payments. That's when vacation homes are shed.

Another underlying driver of the current buyer's market has to do with sellers' motivations. When prices plummet and interest payments go up at the same time, homeowners face a dilemma.

Their payments are rising as their loans roll over to higher rates, but when they try to refinance the loan, they find that their home price has fallen as a result of less demand (caused, in part, by those higher loan rates). The downward cycle has begun, and they are more willing to sell.

The buyer's market, however, will not last forever, even in these real estate trouble zones. The same can be said of the country as a whole. We are going to return to a situation where the banks will resume their role as the lender for businesses and consumers, and Wall Street will pull back a little bit. For commercial projects, there's going to be more equity required; the developer is going to have to have a vested interest; and his track record is going to mean something. For residential mortgages, there will be stricter criteria as well, and borrowers will have to be approved as creditworthy. But banks will lend again.

So if you've got a good income, and a good credit history, now's the time to buy that house. If you've got a questionable credit history, and you're a moderate-income homebuyer, now's the time to go and get that FHA-insured mortgage.

That, by the way, is what people who are wealthy are doing now—buying. The rich get richer because they can pick the opportune time to buy, plus they have access to cash. So now you are going to see the wealthy get wealthier, at the expense of the average person who doesn't recognize a buyer's market. On the bigger playing fields, the subprime mortgage pools and mortgage packages are already getting bought at huge discounts.

Why? Because real estate endures. Historically, when real estate is down, it bounces back, even from recessions and depressions.

Look at New York City in the 1970s. The city was broke; nobody was buying real estate there. Or in the late 1980s—you couldn't give a condo away then. Now condos are selling for as much as $4,500 a square foot. No one would go into Harlem before. Now, brownstones are being sold there for $4 million. The point is that real estate markets always come back, and the key is to look at this current crisis as a buying opportunity. It's what I said in the *Peebles Principles*: Each setback is an opportunity in disguise. This crisis is another opportunity.

Now, you may be concerned that prices are going to fall further. No one can guarantee how bad it's going to get. It may get a little worse after you buy. But if you buy based on where values were, say, five years ago, you really can't go wrong. Yes, prices may drop a little more, but on the flip side you may lose the window of opportunity. The question is how long it will take for the market to get back into balance. Because once that happens, the opportunity is gone.

Have we undergone a national recession? Even if we have, the good thing about real estate, especially housing, is that people need it. Like food, housing is a basic requirement. If you are providing that you have a good investment. Even if we enter a period of economic lethargy, the concomitant fall in housing prices will give you an opportunity to buy the home you couldn't afford before. If you still have your job and your good credit, now you can buy that house for less.

My belief is that we are going to see this opportunity last well into 2009. Then you are going to see the opportunity begin to recede, as we get more into a rising cycle. Because ultimately people are going to need homes, they are going need to relocate, they are going to want to upgrade, and there are going to be new homebuyers coming into the market.

Meanwhile, there is a perception that we are in a nationwide real estate crisis, and that makes it an excellent time to buy. There probably won't be another buying opportunity like this for many years to come.

PART TWO

FUNDAMENTAL TOOLS FOR REAL ESTATE INVESTING

CHAPTER 4

Information Please: Where to Find the Data

The good news about real estate investing is that anyone can do it. Having said that, you need to do your homework to make a superior investment.

Anyone who makes a bet in real estate based purely on gut instincts is flirting with disaster. Not that intuition is without its uses; the annals of real estate fortune-making are replete with stories of investors who apparently shot from the hip, defied logic, and bought at prices or in places that everyone else thought were ridiculous.

The idea that these investors took wild gambles based on some sort of gut feeling is false, however. What actually took place were calculated risks, based on an understanding of the marketplace that was deeper than public perception. As I said previously, if you are going to make money in real estate, that means you have to move at cross currents to the herd mentality. From the outside that looks risky, or even capricious, but when you understand the art of buying well you realize that such investments are far savvier than meet the eye.

Deciding where and when to invest in real estate must be based on knowledge, on doing your homework—finding out as much as you can about the property in question and the market metrics that surround it.

The first order of business is deciding where you want to invest. For some homeowners this is predicated on proximity to family, but for most it's about employment; unless you have a portable job, you want to buy near where you work. A second property is going to have similar constraints. If it's a vacation home, it's where you want to play; if it's an investment property, it should be close or convenient enough to keep on eye on it for maintenance, renting, or renovation.

The first source for what's available in any market is a local realtor. Through their personal contacts, and access to the MLS, or multiple listing services, they should have a pretty good idea of what is out there.

But let's assume you want to do the legwork yourself. A good place to start doing research on available properties is through The National Association of Realtors (NAR), the mother of real estate organizations. Celebrating its 100th anniversary in 2008, NAR is the big national club for real estate professionals.

The web site for NAR is www.realtor.com. Their principle search engine is Find a Home, where you can type in any city in the United States (they have 3 million listings), along with your basic criterion for price range, number of bedrooms, number of baths, and so forth. After it tells you how many properties in that city fit your profile, you can view them as a list or on a map. In either case you can drill down to the details on address, price, bedrooms, bathrooms, square footage, lot size, year built, and other amenities such as fireplace or pool.

Because the data is being fed to the national organization from local or regional realtor organizations, the depth of information varies from state to state. Homes in San Francisco or Los Angeles, for example, can be picked out from a map that also allows you to see a bird's eye aerial view of the property, courtesy of satellite photos from Microsoft Virtual Earth. In Chicago and Denver, however, while there is still a map function, you can't get the bird's eye view photo. Other cities are even less accommodating. Go to Boston, for example, and no maps are available, let alone birds' eye views; even the addresses, except for the neighborhood, are withheld pending a phone call to the realtor for that property. Still, it's a hell of a national database.

For big-picture research from NAR go to their site for the realtors themselves: www.realtor.org. While much of the info here is useless unless you're a realtor (I don't think you really care where this year's meetings and expos will take place), the Research link can be helpful. Here you can find housing statistics, economic indicators, forecasts, and recent research reports by topic. Some of it is quite broad—the shift in median house prices by regions of the United States, for example—but some of it is very concrete, like their annual Profile of Buyers' Home Feature Preferences. Here you can learn what currently turns on homebuyers: central air conditioning versus oversized garages, walk-in closets versus big backyards, hardwood floors versus energy efficiency, and so forth.

The site also has a few academic research reports you can access. One by professors at Florida State University and Middle Tennessee State University looks at how prices are affected by nine variables in the home—stuff like square footage and fireplaces—and how important these are for different parts of the country. A swimming pool most increases home value if you live in the Southwest, for example (fear of the desert, probably), while in the South bigger garages have the biggest bang (room for all that hunting and fishing gear, I suppose).

If it's historic and regional trends that you are interested in, the U.S. Department of Housing and Urban Development, or HUD, keeps the mother lode of such data. Their main site to start your fishing expedition is www.huduser.org, which permits free downloads of more than 1,000 publications and databases. You can also get these reports in hard copy, for a nominal fee, from their HUD User Web Store at www.webstore.huduser.org/catalog.

The most important document you can access is HUD's quarterly report on U.S. Housing Market Conditions. The quarterly report itself contains historical data from the most recent quarter (it lags 90 to 180 days) right back to 1967. It includes charts on housing permits, housing starts, new home sales, existing home sales, average and median prices for new and existing home sales, and so forth. While the national data is atomized only as far as region (Northeast, Midwest, South, and West), it nonetheless provides a great picture of overall trends, and can help you understand how your market compares with the national or regional picture.

Another site you can visit for more current information on the broader market is Microsoft's www.realestate.msn.com, which combines information from several media sources. They can't give you any better listings—their guide to homes for sale comes from Realtor.com—but they will link you to all the recent video segments on real estate from CNBC, as well as to recent *BusinessWeek* articles on the real estate market, accompanied by slide shows.

If you want to narrow your focus geographically, try state realtor associations, like the Illinois Association of Realtors (www.illinoisrealtor.org) or the New York State Association of Realtors (www.nysar.com). If you ask for listings, their sites generally refer you back to the national Realtor database. More useful are the specific stats on the state in question; almost all post quarterly sales and price reports, comparing month-to-month and year-to-year numbers. Some, like the California Association of Realtors (www.car.org), have substantial depth in terms of real estate news and statewide market trends.

The top brokerage companies, like Coldwell Banker andCentury 21, also have comprehensive web sites, with property listings and links to lenders, agents, and more. Century 21 offers CNN-Money.com articles, while Coldwell's site is big on videos, covering everything from how to find a dream home to how to use their 2007 Home Price Comparison Index (a voyeur's platform that lets you see what your home's value would fetch in other places). What such sites do best is to offer well-packaged presentations of properties they are actively listing.

As far as locating properties in areas where you wish to invest, there are also independent regional databases, which can be much richer in terms of their visuals and data details, as well as easier to navigate; they do require contact through the agents, who generally support these sites. A good example is www.homesdatabase.com, which filters data on homes in Virginia, Maryland, West Virginia, the District of Columbia, and Pennsylvania. Here you can search for homes based on broad categories such as bedrooms, baths, price, or zip code (the basic search) or on details such as acreage, year built, proximity to water, style of house, or type of house (the advanced search).

If you find a piece of property that looks interesting, and you want to get more information on what it's all about, the final step is the county assessor's office. These web sites are easily located with any search engine. Their online databases typically use the same kind of satellite imagery as NAR, but the data they supply is deeper. In particular, these sites will tell you who currently owns the property and what they paid for it, along with tax information. They dramatically vary in quality, however, and each county assessor's office web site has different bells and whistles.

Take the Los Angeles County Office of the Assessor, the largest property assessment agency in the nation, covering 2.3 million parcels in a community of 10 million residents. Their Property Assessment Information System (PAIS) lets you search the county for properties by street address, tax ID number, or by street intersection. The properties are displayed as a grid map; click on a given lot, and you get information about the assessed value of the land and the building, the square footage, the tax rate, the homeowners' exemption, and recent sales information (two years back, for that property and anything else within 500 feet).

By comparison, the Cook County Assessor's Office (which covers Chicago), supplies all the same basic information on assessed value, square footage, number of rooms, and so forth, but doesn't supply recent sales information. Instead it offers you their assessment of current market value. It also has something L.A. does not have: a street-level photo of every property listed. Meanwhile, the Washington, D.C., property assessor's data base gives you the owner's name and mailing address online, as well as the price he or she paid for the property; it also gives you the material used for the walls and flooring. It does not, however, give you a photo.

In the end, all of the county assessors nationwide provide the basic information that you need about a particular property. What they don't put online you can sometimes get by phone and, if not, then by visiting a district office. It is all a matter of public record, and you can search through all the past deeds—although going into the historical data may not be that meaningful, unless you want to track property appreciation by price over time. What you want is the state of the current market, and that means what the seller paid. It's generally not realistic to think they will take less than that price, unless it's a distress situation (which may be the case if the property is part of an estate sale or headed for foreclosure.) But, generally speaking, their purchase price is their waterline.

There are other web sites that can be helpful when it comes to tracking data on local and regional housing, and we will look at some of those in other chapters, from data bases that can help you with valuations and trends in neighborhood pricing (Chapter 5) to data bases where you can find properties under foreclosure, slated for auction or owned by banks (Chapter 11). But the ones above are good master sources for locating properties and the basic information on those properties.

Regardless of how much data you are willing to personally mine, however, when it comes to the nitty-gritty of locating homes for sale in your locale, you should still contact a local realtor. Licensed real estate agents have access to the MLS, or Multiple Listing Service, which is a comprehensive database on all properties for sale. It has greater detail and depth than the information available to the public via realtors.com, but you can't use it unless you are a licensed professional; a broker can also pull down other transactional data.

This is why you want to use a broker. Brokers will simply have more information about properties for sale in your neck of the woods than you do. Being in the mix, they are plugged in; they will know the motivation of the seller as well. I can't tell you the number of deals that have come my way, and to people whom I know, through realtors—including that most precious piece of information, a tip about property for sale that has not yet been put on the market. A good broker can feed you opportunities. So

I strongly encourage you to work with an agent that you like and trust.

Now, even though agents can be very helpful in finding property, it is sometimes better to negotiate directly with the seller. You can often get better deals one-on-one, for a variety of reasons—including how your personalities connect. You can do this with your realtor's blessing, or you can reach sellers directly. One way is online; www.craigslist.com, for example, covers about 275 U.S. cities. Their individual city sites all carry owner-posted Real Estate for Sale listings, usually with photos. *When being represented by a broker, however, contacting the seller directly—especially without the broker's knowledge—is not proper etiquette.*

There are a bunch of other sites that also list property posted for sale by its owners, such as owners.com, forsalebyowner.com, fsbo.com, and so forth, each with its own flavor. At buyowner.com, for example, the spin is high-end homes with crisp photography and virtual 360-degree tours you can control with a virtual joystick. Over at homesbyowner.com you get great drill-down maps that go from state to city to neighborhood to street; these are lower-priced houses that come with slide shows and background music.

Don't forget the newspapers, either, which have traditionally carried the residential and commercial real estate listings for their areas of coverage. Classified ads are very localized, and even the smallest ad can lead to an interesting deal; someone who advertises there also probably thinks a little more conservatively than someone online.

This brings us to the final source for finding real estate: being there. Nothing beats being on the street, cruising through neighborhoods that you want to focus on. Everything you see is potentially for sale; it's just a matter price. Has the owner even considered the idea of selling? If a property is not maintained, the owner may not be actively engaged, or may have lost interest in the property, and may be interested in selling. So you do your homework at the county assessor's office, and make an offer.

The important thing here is that once you have found a property that might make a good buy, you have to collect the best information you can to help you negotiate. Nothing beats knowing the particulars of a building or piece of land, including its sales history, its tax payments, the recent sale prices of nearby properties, and so forth. The more data you can gather the better, because there isn't really one source that has it all.

If you do collect all the data, then you can start figuring out what the property is really worth. That comes next.

CHAPTER 5

Adding It Up: A Crash Course in Valuation

Figuring out the value of a piece of property—what it's really worth—is both an analytic and creative process. It is also fundamental to making a good investment.

In the final analysis, building wealth through real estate is all about understanding value. You have to understand how to determine value, and then you have to understand what goes into creating value. These are the two sides of the valuation coin: to get a good sense of what something is worth and then figuring out how to make it worth more.

The first way to create wealth in real estate is to buy well. That is one of the central themes of this book: that you should make your money going into a deal, through buying well. Buying property for less than it's worth creates immediate wealth. The trick is to accurately determine the current—and future—value of the property in question.

The other way to make money in real estate is to unlock value through creativity. By that I mean taking property and transforming it in some way to make it more valuable. This can take the form of anything from putting in the right upgrades on residential housing to subdividing a large parcel of land and selling off the pieces at higher prices per square foot.

But let's start with making money through buying well.

What determines the value of any given piece of property? How do you know how much it is worth? The simplest answer is that any piece of property is worth whatever someone else is willing to pay for it. While this is an accurate (if somewhat facetious) statement, it still does not give you a yardstick or methodology to benchmark the price that someone might be willing to pay.

The people whose job it is to determine the current value of real estate are the professional appraisers, and they are licensed by exam on a state-by-state basis. I started my real estate career as an appraiser back in 1979. Assuming that you do not intend to become a professional appraiser yourself, it might still be valuable to either read an appraisal book or take an appraisal class, because these teach you the fundamentals of valuation. For me, this knowledge became the foundation of my investment decisions, and I rely upon it to this day.

A good place to look for classes or texts is through the Appraisal Institute (www.appraisalinstitute.org), which has state chapters in many part of the country. They offer a catalogue of classes, but the relevant one for the beginning investor is their Basic Appraisal Principles, a four-day course held in cities like Tampa, Knoxville, New York, San Diego, Chicago, and so forth. It costs between $400 and $500, depending on location. They sell a basic textbook, as well, the Appraisal of Real Estate, which you can order online for $75.

There are also online courses you can take to learn about the basics of appraisal, and some offer sufficient curriculum to take you all the way to your state exam for licensing. You can scour the Web for these, and if you have any questions regarding their legitimacy, you can contact the National Association of Real Estate Appraisers (www.narea-assoc.org).

Without going into excruciating detail, what most appraisal courses will teach you is that there are different ways to figure out the real value of property. The three basic methods are the comparable sales approach to value, the replacement cost approach to value, and, if you are looking at buying for the purpose of renting, the income approach to value.

The comparable sales approach to value is essentially a market approach, using current market data, and basing value on the principle of substitution. The theory is that buyers are not going to pay you more for a house than they would for a comparable house in the same or a similar neighborhood. This is why you go to the county assessor offices that we discussed in the last chapter. You need to check and see what people have been paying for similar houses in the neighborhood, especially in terms of price per square foot.

The replacement cost approach to value is just that—what it would cost to replace the house, plus the value of the land. This approach is most reliable when evaluating newly constructed properties. For older homes, county assessor offices break down valuation in terms of land and building, but these figures are usually quite understated if the house has not changed hands in a while. For the sake of tax assessments, properties are typically valued much closer to their original purchase price than to their current value, a methodology intended to keep neighborhoods stable as prices rise (otherwise limited-income homeowners in areas that jump in taxable value would be forced to relocate). A better source of information on construction costs is Marshall & Swift (www. marshallswift.com), the firm that produces the industry standard commercial Marshall Valuation Service. A less expensive version for your purposes is their *Residential Cost Handbook*; they offer on-line appraisal classes as well. You can also keep tabs on costs through construction industry cost reports.

The finer tuning on the replacement cost approach takes into consideration the cost of improvements to an existing property, and then calculates the depreciated value of those improvements, plus profit and overhead for the builder. The idea is that no one is going to pay significantly more than what it costs to build something. They will pay 10 to 15 percent more (fluctuating based upon demand) because they can have the property right away; buyers may pay more than the dollar cost of installing central air conditioning, for example, since they won't have to endure the construction process. But they are not going to pay 25 to 50 percent more. Nonetheless, when it comes to existing homes, these adjustments become more subjective, and so the cost approach becomes a less reliable indication of value than it is for newly constructed properties.

Then there is the income approach, which is most reliable for commercial properties whose purpose it is to generate income for its owner. It essentially values a property based on its income earning potential. This is appropriate if you are looking at small apartment buildings or small storefront retail buildings, right up to large shopping malls, hotels, and large office buildings. It will require you to understand the true income potential of the building—its operating expenses versus its rental rates.

In the event you are purchasing a vacant property, you will have to do a survey of comparable asking and existing rental rates for similar properties. In the event the property is currently leased you must review the leases as well as the operating expense history of the property. Areas of focus should be the remaining term of the lease(s), what operating expenses the renter pays, and whether the rents are likely to increase, hold steady, or decline upon lease expiration(s). This will give you an indication of your potential investment risk; naturally, if rents are projected to go lower, then your risk is significantly increased. The next step is to analyze the cost of debt service, taxes, improvements, maintenance, and so forth, and weigh these against what you can charge current and future tenants. These factors must be considered when making a determination of price and whether or not to buy.

You can also try to look at single-family homes as rental opportunities. But it is harder to make such investments work. It is generally difficult to command enough in rental payments to cover debt service and operating expenses on single-family houses. On the other hand, the best chance you will have to do so is when the market pulls back significantly. What's happening now is that values are going down and rents are moving up, so the current market might open a window for this; certainly if you can make these numbers work for a single-family home, then you have a strong measure of value.

Now, obsessed as the United States is with real estate values and homeownership, you would think that information on home valuations would be available in some vast database. It is. Several web sites offer to tell you what your home is worth, based on their own secret algorithms and proprietary data. One of the more popular and interesting is Zillow.com, which is also filled with an omnibus of real estate advice—much of it obvious and common sense based, with lots of commentary by single homebuyers in the style of Wikipedia.

What is most interesting for our purposes is what the site calls its "Zestimate" of home values (you got it, rhymes with estimate), which uses their proprietary formula to estimate the market value of 70 million homes in the United States. The fun part is that, using satellite photography images, you can zoom in on most houses in the country, especially those in towns and cities (they are a little spottier when it comes to rural homes). Even if you don't know the exact address you can request the name of a street in any given city, then just tool around until you find the home you are looking for. The Zestimate is right there on the property, just as it is on every other house on the block.

Of course, as Zillow points out, these are just estimates and not appraisals. In order to get a more precise valuation, the site suggests you visit the house, get a Comparative Market Analysis (CMA) from a real estate agent, get a professional appraisal, and, finally, figure out the estimate yourself, based on special features, location, market conditions, and so forth. This last part is important, because while value is determined by comparable pricing trends and replacement costs, it is also influenced by a host of other things, from the tiny (such as what fixtures are in the master bathroom) to the global (such as the national perception of where real estate is going).

When I started in real estate, my first job was as an appraisal trainee working for my mother, who was an independent fee appraiser with HUD as her largest client. Essentially we were appraising low- and moderate-income homes in and around Washington, D.C. I would make our estimate based on a checklist of criteria. Among them were previous sale prices for the home in question and the sale prices of similar houses in the neighborhood. But then it came down to details about the condition of the house, the amenities it had, and so forth. Sometimes small details can have a big impact. The value of these items was always somewhat subjective.

Parenthetically, the good news about appraising, and having an understanding of valuation, is that you can use those skill sets in any real estate market around the country—or the world, for that matter. That's how I got into other markets after I honed my appraisal skills in Washington, because I understood the concept of how to estimate value and how to create value. And those skills are not tied to any given location.

Now, having discussed these investigative and observational methods of figuring out what real estate is worth, there is another, simpler way to look at the value of property in the current down market. Perhaps the most surefire way to value a given property is to look at what it was worth before the big up-tick in the marketplace. What was the property worth in 2000? What was it worth in 2002? What was it worth five years ago? If you can buy a property for what it was worth then, you are pretty safe.

You are safe because we know historically that real estate, after the current downturn, is going to come back to its former value and eventually go beyond that. And if you can buy based on five-year-old prices, then that's going to be at maybe half the peak value. In such cases you don't even need to wait for the price to return to its peak in order to make a strong return on your investment. Recover half the difference, and you've still made a lot of money. Recover a third of what was lost, and you still make a significant profit.

Think about this for a minute. Say you buy a property that was worth $300,000 dollars six months ago, or eight months ago, or a year ago. Five years back say it was worth $150,000, or maybe even $200,000. If you can buy that house for $200,000 today, you don't need it to go back to $300,000 before you make money. If you can sell it for $250,000, you've made 25 percent on the whole cost if you paid cash. If you leveraged the purchase, and put down 10 percent, then you invested $20,000. Therefore if you clear $50,000, you are taking a return of about 150 percent on your investment. Even spread out over a couple of years, that is a phenomenal return, especially in view of the fact that at any time over the past 10 years it has been difficult to get more than 3 percent from a bank money market account.

Now, by and large, at least on a macro level, real estate prices in the United States have not yet returned to where they were five years ago. As of early 2008, prices were still about 30 percent higher than what they were at the beginning of of 2003. So, you are going to have to pay below current prices if you want to get that really spectacular deal. And that should be no surprise. If everyone could buy at prices from five years ago, then everybody would be wealthy. But that's not the case.

An interesting site to go to for benchmarking prices from five years ago, by the way, is www.trulia.com. It's a comprehensive real estate site, with databases of houses for sale, and an interesting "heat map" feature that lets you look at metropolitan areas that are color coded for the hottest submarkets in terms of pricing (the hotter the color, the higher the asking price).

What's most helpful in this context is their section on local real estate data. You can go to any city, and the data for that market is broken down into average sales price, median sales price, average price per square foot, and number of sales. The numbers are presented as quarterly spreads (November 2007 through January 2008, for example) and then compared to the numbers in the previous quarter, the year before quarter, and the quarter from five years before. Each category also offers up a chart that tracks the prices back to January 1, 2000.

One look at this and you realize how far prices have come in the last half decade. Let's take Phoenix, for example. The average sales price of a home in that market rose from $163,277 in late 2002 to just over $400,000 at the peak. As of the first quarter of 2008, the average sale price had receded to $245,381. That price represents a 22.2 percent slide from the previous quarter in 2007, and an 18.3 percent drop compared to a year earlier. Compared to late 2002, however, the price was still up by 50 percent. This means that Phoenix still has a ways to go, especially with an inventory of 54,000 houses in March of 2008, up from 47,500 a year earlier.

Individual neighborhoods can reveal another story, of course, and can deviate from the broader trends. The average sales price for a home in Los Angeles at the end of the first quarter of 2008, for example, was 54 percent above its price five years earlier. But specific neighborhoods differed. The average sale price for homes in Silver Lake, a gentrifying community near downtown, was still up 63.5 percent from five years earlier; homes in posh Bel Air were still up 172 percent from five years earlier. So while statistics are macro, individual investments remain micro.

Here is a good example. My company is developing projects in the San Francisco Bay area, and as a result I am required to spend considerable time in the area. In the summer of 2005, my wife and I decided to look for a house. We spent several weeks reviewing reports and brochures for scores of properties, and after physically inspecting several dozen decided to buy a home in a suburban community called Hillsborough. We found a house that was listed for $12 million but decided it was too expensive. When we found it was still on the market a year later, however, we put it under contract for $9,500,000. When an inspection revealed a few problems, we insisted the sellers pay for repairs; when they refused (it was still a seller's market then), we terminated our contract. Amazingly enough, the house was still on the market the following summer of 2007; we offered $7.5 million, but the seller would not go below $7.8 million. Someone finally bought the house in December

2007 for $6.7 million! As they say, you've got to know when to hold and when to fold. Had the sellers made the deal with us even in 2007 they would have made $800,000 more. This is also an example of how a seller's motivation influences price. In this case the sellers were divorcing and one party wanted to move on quickly while the other was stalling. Ultimately they both decided to move on, so the party who finally bought the house made a great deal.

So, though we are experiencing a clearing out of inventory, and values are pulling back, most have not yet returned to where they were five years earlier. If you are patient, however, there are great opportunities; you just have to search below the surface and remember in this market no offer is too low or insulting.

The other way to build wealth in real estate, as we discussed, is to create value. This has been one of the fundamental ways in which I've created a fortune in real estate. If you look at my major deals, which I detail in my book *The Peebles Principles*, many of them made their stellar returns because of the value that I unlocked in the property.

In Washington, for example, most of the profits that I made were because I bought when the market was way, way down. The value of the building that I bought at 900 F Street, however, was hugely increased by creative enhancement. First, I was able to get historic tax credits for the structure, which had been a Riggs Bank building a century earlier. I then transformed the building from office to hospitality; as a Courtyard Marriott its cash flow increased dramatically.

I did the same with the Bath Club in Miami Beach. First, I was able to buy for a low price, based on my commitment to preserving the historic Bath Club for its owners and members. Then I was able to rezone the remaining land for a midsized condo, which dramatically increased the value of the property. I also had the historic club house designated a historic landmark, which made it eligible for historic tax credits.

In both these examples I was able to use the two approaches to realizing value, first through buying low, and then by creatively unlocking value—in these cases by changing usage. That is what you need to see when you are trying to create new value: the highest and best usage for a piece of property. If you can see that, where someone else cannot, then you will do well.

This concept of changing usage may not be possible for non-commercial, individual homes. But you can still enhance a property's value, especially if you understand what contributes to that—what people want and what the market will pay for certain improvements. The market may not pay more for wallpaper, but it may pay much more for solid wood doors. The market may not pay more for pavers, but it may pay more for landscaping. When you understand what the market is going to pay for something, then you will know what the potential is for any given piece of property, and what you should focus on when it comes time to renovate, make additions, or upgrade the property in other ways. You will also know what not to pay a premium for when you are buying something yourself.

Knowing what works and what doesn't work is partly a matter of your personal field research—just looking at houses that recently sold and why they sold for the price they did. You can also find research on buyer preferences in some of the data sources we mentioned in the previous chapter. The best source, however, may still be that local realtor we also discussed. A typical realtor will probably see more houses in a month than you'll see in a lifetime. Realtors will know better than anyone what features are selling homes in your neighborhood. These range from the obvious (a fresh coat of paint, new bathroom fixtures and handsome-looking windows are almost always winners, for instance) to the not so obvious (replacing refrigerators, stoves, and dishwashers sometimes produce no gain, since the kitchen is the first place most people want to renovate to their tastes).

Something else you want to pay attention to is the most recent inspection of the property, for either buying or selling. On the buying side, you can probably negotiate $2 to $3 dollars off the price for every dollar that you think it will take to repair some obvious fault. On the selling side, replacing or repairing something essential, like a roof or a furnace, enhances value beyond the dollar investment, since for the buyer it means no hassles. More subtly, it shows that the seller has maintained the house well.

Just remember that there is a certain level of improvement above which you will see no return. If you are in a neighborhood where there is a price ceiling, and you put in an extra level of finishes, you can say goodbye to that investment. In given price ranges there are buyers who are not discerning enough, or who can't afford the extra cost, because the market is sealed down, topped out. So when you try to create value, understand first what the market will or will not pay for.

In the meantime, you should be waiting and watching as house prices decline. Will they fall substantially further? If the answer to that is yes, then the question becomes "when will the misery index fall far enough to where you can start buying?" Again, I think you've definitely hit bottom when prices get back down to 2002 or 2003 prices. If prices drop to that level, you are going to see buying opportunities everywhere. Another way to sound out the bottom is to keep an eye on inventories. When they return to the level of a nine-month supply, that means excess product is being absorbed and prices are stabilizing; and when they reach a six-month supply, that means prices will start to rise again, and it's probably too late to get the steals.

Regardless of when you buy, understanding how to appraise the value of a house is a very valuable tool in becoming a real estate entrepreneur, or making money in the real estate business. Otherwise you've got to rely on other people's estimates, and they may be wrong. Plus, armed with this knowledge, you will be able to act quickly to take advantage of opportunities when they present themselves. Others may have underestimated or overestimated the worth of a property, and neither one of these are good things. It's better to have a strong sense of value yourself.

If you can identify value, then you can make decisions with a sense of guidance. Without that you will be like a rudderless ship.

CHAPTER 6

The Big Guns: Finding Help from the Government

*If you want to buy property, or protect property that is
now threatened by skyrocketing mortgage payments,
don't discount the power of government programs.*

The United States is one of the best-housed countries in the world.
From a low of 40 percent of all households during the Great Depression, to a high of more than 68 percent of households today,
America is a land of homeowners. Owning the roof over your head
is a fundamental part of the American Dream.

One of the big catalysts for this expansion of home ownership has been the Federal Housing Administration, more commonly called the FHA, which was created in 1934 by the federal government as a way to help low- and moderate-income families afford housing during the Depression.

The way it works is simple. The FHA guarantees the mortgage you get from the bank. This encourages banks to lend you money, because if you fail to make the payments and your home goes into foreclosure, the federal government will pay off the bank. In essence, the FHA acts like a mortgage insurance company. Since its inception, it's insured more than 34 million home mortgages and 47,000 multifamily housing mortgages. Today its portfolio includes 4.8 million single-family homes and 13,000 multifamily projects.

Many people think the FHA serves only first-time homebuyers, but that is not the case. Anyone can qualify, as long as they meet a short list of requirements. These include verification of current income; two-years' worth of verifiable income; and proof, through your credit report, that two years have passed since a bankruptcy, and three years since a foreclosure. There is no minimum income required as long as your monthly housing costs don't exceed 31 percent of that income, and as long as all long-term debt service combined (house plus car payments, for instance) does not exceed 43 percent of that income.

In the pros and cons department, the pros of an FHA-backed loan are that you only need to put down 3 percent, and your bank (you still have to get your mortgage through a bank) will be a lot more lenient with you on things like your credit rating, because they are off the hook if you falter. The biggest con is that, until early in 2008, the maximum loan amount was $362,790, and this was for high-cost areas like Westchester County outside of New York City. Now, emergency federal legislation has upped that to $729,750, but only for the high-cost areas and only until the end of 2008. The basic standard is just $271,050 for "normal markets" (though you can get a fair amount of housing for that in a city like Cleveland).

There are two other things of interest. One is FHA's 203(k) program, also known as the Rehabilitation Loan Program, which lets you borrow the money you need to fix up a property, and includes that amount as part of the loan; the cap is currently $35,000.

The other thing is that you can get an FHA-backed loan for purchasing multifamily housing. As an individual you can buy a building with up to four units; the maximum loan amount goes up with each additional unit, capping out at $697,696 for a four-unit building. What's great about this is that you can include the rents you'll be collecting as part of the income that you need to qualify for FHA approval.

The FHA will also insure loans for larger buildings, under their 207 and 221 programs. These work in a similar fashion to the single-family mortgage insurance program, except that they cover only 90 percent of the appraised value of the project unless you are a nonprofit, in which case they'll go up to 100 percent. The properties can also be owned by partnerships, groups of investors, and so forth, so you can benefit from your partners' higher credit ratings. Again, there are caps to the amount they will insure, a number that varies from area to area. The basic rule of thumb is that the building includes five or more rentable units; buildings with four units or less are considered single residential properties.

Since 1965, the FHA has been part of the U.S. Department of Housing and Urban Development, a cabinet-level department of the federal government, commonly referred to by its acronym HUD. It was established by President Lyndon Johnson as part of his Great Society mission to revitalize the urban centers of U.S. cities, which were being abandoned for the suburbs. Over the years HUD has shifted its focus more toward housing, though it's still active on the urban development front with programs like its Community Development Block Grants.

For our purposes, HUD's value is that it's the place where FHA homes and multifamily housing end up after they've been foreclosed (they also get foreclosed Veterans Administration homes, so-called VA mortgages, which are backed similar to FHA loans but are only for veterans). After paying off the bank that made the FHA- or VA-insured loan, HUD owns the home and sells it as a way of recovering its loss on the foreclosure.

Just about anyone can buy a HUD property, but the first priority goes to buyers who intend to occupy the home as their primary residence. Properties in certain designated economic development areas are offered at reduced prices for municipal employees, such as police officers, teachers, firefighters, emergency medical personnel, and other government and nonprofit employees who intend to live there. Following a specified period of time, if no prospective homeowner buys the property, then an investor can take a shot.

The properties available for sale are listed on the Internet, on sites that are maintained by management companies under contract with HUD. You will need to use a licensed real estate broker registered with HUD to submit a bid, but HUD pays the real estate broker's commission. All properties are sold as-is, with no warranties, so you had better inspect the property first.

A recent tour of the HUD site (www.hud.gov) led us to search the "HUD home" link, and from there, the listings for Ohio. We looked at a typical example: a 4-bed, 2-bath split-level house in Chesterland, a suburb of Cleveland. This home, with fireplace and two-car garage, was appraised in August 2007 at $188,000. It was offered for sale at $160,000. Another, a 1925 Colonial style house in Cincinnati with porch, balcony, and fireplace, had been appraised at $84,000 in October 2007. It was being offered at $77,000. It had 16 rooms, including 4 bedrooms and 4 bathrooms.

Once you decide you want to buy a HUD home, you submit your bid (via a real estate agent) during the "Offer Period."

At the end of that period all the bids are opened and the highest bid—assuming that it comes within spitting distance of the asking price—wins. If the home is not sold during that time, the bid period is extended, usually on a daily basis, until an acceptable bid is received.

HUD does not guarantee anything about the property you buy. But they do have a bunch of special programs that can help, including allowances to pay for moving expenses, bonuses for early closings, or help towards upgrading the property (part of the above-mentioned rehab program). Again, if you are a municipal employee such as a firefighter or school teacher and buy a HUD home in a specially designated "revitalization area," you are entitled to a 50 percent discount on the list price for the property. The principal requirement is that you commit to living there for three years; this program, like others at HUD, is intended to rebuild the urban core.

As long as we are discussing federal housing and mortgage programs, you may as well be familiar with Fannie Mae and Freddie Mac.

Fannie Mae is shorthand for the Federal National Mortgage Association, another Depression-era federal creation. Part of FDR's New Deal, it was founded in 1938 to pump liquidity into the mortgage market. It did this, and still does, by purchasing mortgages from banks and other lenders, and repackaging these loans as mortgage-backed securities. Fannie Mae guarantees these bonds, and that's how it makes money: by charging a fee for the guarantee.

Fannie Mae was privatized in 1968 to help balance the federal budget, but since it consequently held a virtual monopoly on the secondary mortgage market, the government chartered a competitor, the Federal Home Loan Mortgage Corporation, a.k.a. *Freddie Mac*. It pretty much does the same thing as Fannie Mae.

Two things about Fannie and Freddie you should know. The first is that they will buy only what are known as conforming loans.

These are loans that follow certain criteria, including proper debt-to-income ratios on the part of the borrowers. They are also capped based on annual changes in the mean price of homes, and they have had the same ceiling since 2006—$417,000—except for an exception established by the economic stimulus package of early 2008. Under this legislation, Frannie and Freddie could both guarantee "jumbo-conforming" loans of up to $729,750 in certain high-priced cities until the end of the year.

The jumbo reference was formerly reserved for amounts above the conforming limit of $417,000. Anything above this was a called a jumbo loan. The effect for consumers was that jumbo loans charged higher interest rates, typically a quarter to a half a percent surcharge (and sometimes more), since they could not be sold as easily on the secondary market. Banks still do charge higher rates if the loan amount exceeds the cap of $729,750 for the jumbo-conforming loan.

The other thing to know about Fannie and Freddie is that while they are both "government-sponsored enterprises," or GSEs, the federal government does not back them financially. While they do enjoy the support of the government and have certain privileges, both Fannie Mae and Freddie Mac are publicly traded corporations. Technically speaking they could fail; though it's unlikely the federal government would allow that to happen, and the standard thinking in economic circles is that an implicit government guarantee exists for Fannie and Freddie.

The reason the federal government would never let either of these giant GSEs go down is the same reason that the government is now engaged in various programs to stave off the sub-prime mortgage disaster. Having seen the turmoil—and subsequent recession—created by the downward spiral of real estate prices in the early 1990s, the government does not want to let a similar scenario unfold. If housing prices decline too sharply, the people who took out all those mortgages at close-to-value could panic; if this herd starts to stampede, you will see many more foreclosures than the million predicted for 2008. Even if all these borrowers can afford their mortgage payments, nothing puts a damper on consumer confidence like owing more than a home is worth.

So the government will be doing as much as possible to prevent a panic, on both the federal and local levels. You can see this in some of the programs already trotted out. In late 2007 the federal government hammered out a deal with the major lenders to freeze interest rates for a portion of the homeowners holding subprime loans. Realizing the inadequacy of this effort, the government came back in early 2008 with Project Lifeline, a program to put foreclosures on hold for 30 days in order to help homeowners work out solutions with their lenders.

Unlike the first effort, Project Lifeline included all residential mortgage holders (not just subprime), and was backed by the top six banks that, collectively, service half of all U.S. mortgages. While it presents little more than a hiatus for troubled homeowners, any delay could help; the U.S. prime rate was already back down to 5 percent in early 2008—at least three points lower than most of 2006 and 2007—which opens the door to lower payments for homeowners who can negotiate deals with their banks.

These sorts of programs are going to become more widespread in 2008 and 2009, although they will be less helpful to you as an investor than as a mortgagee in trouble (a situation we will address in the last chapters of this book). Even if you are not in dire straits, however, these programs could present opportunities to refinance your mortgage for a lower rate.

The big event that could prove to be a boon for such refinancing is making permanent the elevation of the ceiling for conforming loans at Fannie Mae and Freddie Mac. If HUD permits—and

Congress enacts—the package floated in early 2008 for Fannie and Freddie could permanently guarantee loans for as much as $729,750, thereby allowing banks to finance bigger loans at lower rates. The measure is designed to pump liquidity into a credit-thirsty system; the runoff might open up some possibilities for you.

Much of the help from the government during these days of growing inventory and falling prices will arise on a more local level. Cities and counties nationwide are concerned that the rising flood of foreclosures will leave certain neighborhoods strewn with abandoned properties. Once that sort of rot sets in, prices could spiral even lower, impacting the economic well-being of homeowners still in place.

One solution that counties and cities are turning to is the creation of land banks, in which local governments buy vacant homes and sell them to low-income homeowners (as opposed to speculators or slum lords). In California, for instance, the San Diego Reinvestment Task Force is pushing a plan for the city to purchase houses priced under $400,000 that have been on the market for six months or more. They would then offer these properties at reduced rates to teachers, municipal workers, and low-income residents.

Similar efforts are under way in cities as diverse as Providence, Rhode Island, and Flint, Michigan. These kinds of programs could be helpful if you intend to occupy the property you buy. They are worth checking out in your area.

Keep in mind, however, that the programs you're going to want to focus on are those from the FHA, simple programs that are right online, because they're going to be the ones most forgiving on credit. Fannie Mae and Freddie Mac are conventional financing tools, and the loans they back pretty much need unblemished credit. The good news is that, as Fannie and Freddie raise their limits, the FHA should follow, since its loan limits are tied to a percentage of the Freddie and Fannie caps. If this happens, then you are talking about some real opportunity. In the meantime, keep on eye on communities with home ownership assistance programs, where they'll allow low down payments, and so forth, especially for municipal and workforce employees.

In the end, the federal government will back these local programs. HUD alone has $5.5 billion in block-grant funding for 2008, which can be applied to community programs and other housing issues. More programs will emerge as well, because housing is just too important for the economy. If you think about it, our national economic dependence on housing is probably a scary thing. But that's why the government will intervene, and help you survive—or make money—even in the worst of times.

One of the key lessons in my first book, *The Peebles Principles*, is that setbacks yield opportunities. In the current mortgage crisis, there are plenty of both.

CHAPTER 7

Money Talks: Negotiating with the Lender

The average person who goes to a bank for a mortgage figures it's not negotiable. Wrong. Here are a few helpful insights to help you negotiate with the man behind the curtain.

Bankers are not priests. Yet most people who visit banks or lenders for their home mortgages—partly because it's the biggest investment they will likely make in their lifetimes—treat the banker and institution with a reverence normally reserved for someone in a holy role.

You need to get over that. Banks and mortgage companies are businesses, and frankly they need you more than you need them. They want, and need, to lend you money, just as car dealers need to sell you cars. Just like car dealers, the prices they charge are negotiable. Quite simply, they are in the money renting business, and just like with a landlord, the rental rate and other terms can be modified.

The average person who goes to a bank for a mortgage doesn't understand that. Everybody knows you can bargain for cars, but people don't understand how much you can bargain on real estate loans. When I've done mortgages on my houses, I've negotiated payment terms, rate, structure, and so forth. Sometimes you can't negotiate all of the terms you want. But there are plenty of ways to work out a more advantageous plan, and you have more leverage than you think.

Perhaps I am simply more used to the game. In developing commercial real estate, which is my business, you see that everything is negotiable, and that loans are restructured all the time. Look at the career of Donald Trump; he is a case study in the art of restructuring loans, both to take advantage of better rates when the prime shifts downward, and to get himself out of trouble when a deal is not working well.

There are three times when you want to negotiate with your banker. The first time is when you are going into the mortgage. That's what we will look at here. The second is when you are buying bank-owned property, which we will look at in Chapter 11. The third is when your mortgage is in trouble, and that we will cover in Chapter 14.

When you apply for a new loan, the banker you are generally dealing with is a loan officer, who is essentially a loan salesperson. In fact, loan officers are typically compensated based upon performance—the number of loans they close. They are focused primarily on that objective. The loan goes next to the underwriter, the person who usually evaluates your application. The underwriter is really concerned only with a couple of things. First and foremost, does the property appraise out at an equal or greater value than the purchase price? The next and equally important factors are the quality of your credit and the quantity of your down payment.

These last are also your two best negotiating tools, because they are the two biggest things that impact the risk of the loan. If you have a great track record of paying your bills on time, then you are likely to continue doing so in the future. And if you put a hefty amount of the price down in cash, not only does that make you less likely to walk away from the property, it gives the bank greater asset value should they ever foreclose.

The only other thing that compares to the power of credit and cash is when you are buying a piece of property at a price well below appraised value. This gives the bank a great sense of comfort, since they'd have a valuable asset if you defaulted. This is hard to do, however, unless you are purchasing the property under distress conditions, where the seller is forced to sell quickly, or if it's a property that has been foreclosed on by its lender.

Buying below appraised value can also occur if you have contracted for a price prior to the appraisal of land or building, and/or the seller had no idea what the property was really worth when he signed a contract to sell it to you. In rapidly declining markets the opportunity to purchase properties below appraised value will present itself when markets are being unfairly penalized, in spite of good fundamentals, and both buyers and sellers are panicking. In other cases the appraised value at the time of contract may change prior to closing—if you have an option on the property, for example, and then get it rezoned before you close (something we look at in Chapter 12).

These aside, your best tools are credit and cash, and there should be an inverse relationship between the amount of either and the rates and fees that you are charged.

The first step in the process is to speak with a loan officer at a bank or a mortgage broker if you want to borrow through a mortgage company. You should get an initial proposal, hopefully in the form of a commitment letter. Now, in the normal course of buying a home this is when people succumb to a euphoric mood, happy to have their dream house within grasp. But, as I've said before, emotion is the worst thing when it comes to buying a house. Never get emotional when buying real estate—it impairs your judgment! You need to be dispassionate, and use this commitment letter purely as the starting point.

Basically, you want to see what other banks will offer to sweeten the deal. In fact, you should probably apply for a mortgage with a few different lenders from the outset, to see who makes the best first offer. Then you can take the best back to the rest and see how much they want to compete for your business. If you use a mortgage broker they can do this for you; their job is to represent your interests and get you the best deal. They are transaction oriented, however; so you will likely need to push them to pursue several loan proposals aggressively. If you plan on going to the banks yourself, you should contact several; many times, you can make your applications over the Internet. I strongly recommend that you engage a mortgage broker, as they will have broad access to the most active and aggressive lenders in your community. Whichever lender you approach, always remember this: they can be flexible (up to a point) on rates, fees, and terms. All are negotiable.

One of our company's employees, for example, recently moved to Las Vegas to help oversee a major project we are developing there. I encouraged him to talk to a couple of the bankers we do business with, to get different proposals. In the end he got his lender down a full point on interest rates, and also got them to agree to wave their loan fees. He actually got a better rate than several of the commercial banks with which our company does tens of millions of dollars in business.

You may not want to do the negotiating yourself. Most people are uncomfortable negotiating, because most people are conflict adverse, and they see negotiating as something of a conflict. The mortgage banker or broker is one option, since they will do the talking for you; another option is to use online services like LendingTree.com or BankRate.com, which take your information and farm it out to different banks and mortgage companies in order to bring you the best offer.

You can easily negotiate with your lender directly, however, and use these services as another negotiating tool; at bankrate.com, for example, you can get the latest national overnight averages for things like 30-year fixed-rate mortgages, as well as predictions from mortgage experts as to the direction that rates are going. Then all you have to do is tell your lender that you have an offer from another bank, and ask them if they can beat it. Just because this may be the biggest investment of your life doesn't mean you need to be intimidated when it comes to asking for a better deal. It should be just the opposite.

In terms of specifics, what you are really looking for from the bank are better rates or better terms, or both. On rates, try to get them to give you a point or two off the going mortgage rate. Banks typically tack three points on to the rate at which they borrow money from the Federal Reserve, so they may be able to go below the current mortgage rate—especially if the Fed is trending downward. On terms, where you really want them to back off are on the "points" they charge for the loan. Points are another way of saying percentage, and each point the bank charges you—basically for the privilege of lending you the money—equals 1 percent of the purchase price. That's $2,000 for each point on a $200,000 mortgage, and they can ask for several points. You should be able to get these shaved or eliminated. You can also ask the bank to reduce the settlement costs, which can add up to another couple of points; or you may want to push the envelope in terms of lower initial interest rates, or percentage down.

There are a couple of things to keep in mind when negotiating directly with a banker. While being humble and not cocky (bankers can have inflated egos), you should still maintain the stance that you can always go to another banker if he or she doesn't make you a great deal. Also, as in any negotiation, you should ask for more than you expect to get, so the banker can feel that he or she won a few points and did a good job for the employer. And, just as it helps in negotiating with a seller, it's good to be prequalified to borrow at a certain level. This gives you credibility in the negotiation.

Prequalification also gives you something else, which we will talk about more in Chapter 11: the power to close and the power to close quickly. That can be helpful when dealing with bankers as well as with sellers. In the case of bank-owned property, which we will also talk about in Chapter 11, the power to close quickly can be a clincher. The home in Potomac that I bought in 1995 had been taken back by First Union Bank. It was listed at $3 million, and I made an offer of $1 million. We went back and forth until they agreed to sell it to me for $1.25 million, but only if I could close by the (fast-approaching) end of the year. They wanted to close out their books. We sold the property three years later for $1.6 million.

There are two other points to keep in mind. One is that it doesn't matter whether property is rising or falling in value, whether it's a seller's or buyer's market. Lenders need the business in both scenarios. The other point is a concept close to the core of the negotiating process: when to accept "no" and when not to accept "no." Without going into detail here, the best advice is to not accept the first couple of nos. For further advice, you will have to wait for my next book, on the art of negotiating.

In the meantime, just realize that with solid credit and some cash, now is a great time to negotiate a good deal from a lender. Lenders should give you better rates and easier terms for a high credit score or more money down. The amount you can save has no statutory regulations and is based on individual business decisions. These can vary. It's a game, and if you look at it that way, it can be fun to play. Remember, banks want to lend you money. That's the business they are in. Your objective is to borrow it as cheaply as you can.

PART THREE

CREATING WEALTH IN THE NEW LANDSCAPE

CHAPTER 8

Boom to Bust: Making Money in Down Times

*To understand the current situation you have
to look back at historic real estate cycles, in particular
to the real estate crisis of the early 1990s.*

My best analogy for understanding how the real estate cycle works is to think of it as a 12-hour clock, with 12 o'clock being the peak of the market. Basically, you want to be a buyer from 5 o'clock to 9 o'clock, and you want to be a seller from 11 o'clock to 12 o'clock. Between the hours of 12 and 5, and between 9 and 11, you want to be a spectator.

The trick is knowing what time it is. That's the first trick, anyway. The next trick is having the stomach to buy when most people don't want to buy; that's when the most money is made.

If getting rich were as easy as follow the leader, then we'd have a whole society of rich people. But rich people tend to be eccentric; they go out of step with the average person. Rich people also tend to be cocky, because they think of themselves as different. And they are. They move against the herd. In real estate investing you have to do the same. When everyone else is buying that's the worst time to buy, and when fewer people are buying and lots of people are trying to sell, that's the best time to buy.

This becomes evident when you look at who made money and who lost money in previous U.S. real estate cycles, especially during the down side—between 5 o'clock and 9 o'clock—which is when buyers make their money.

The most recent real estate bust prior to the current meltdown, and one of the easiest to understand, was the one that took place in the late 1980s and early 1990s. This was the so-called S&L crisis, in which the real estate collapse was driven by a banking crisis, in particular by the spectacular failure of savings and loan associations all across the country.

Savings and loan associations have been part of the American financial landscape since the early 1800s. They are primarily community-based institutions designed to help local citizens with savings and mortgages. That, at least, has been their traditional role.

In the late 1970s the S&Ls in this country went through a tough time, thanks to inflation and rising interest rates that sapped their profits and drained their deposits. Because their money was tied up in long-term mortgages with low fixed interest rates, their assets became less valuable as market rates rose. Tight regulations also capped the rate of return they could offer depositors. By 1981, 3,300 of the nation's 3,500 S&Ls were losing money.

The federal government decided to intervene, and although its intentions were good, it overreacted to the situation. In 1982

Congress passed legislation that let S&Ls do all sorts of things they couldn't do before, with the idea of making them more competitive. Overnight, S&Ls were allowed to pay higher market rates for deposits, make commercial loans, take ownership positions in real estate projects they were financing, purchase junk bonds, and more.

The effect was like letting a genie out of the bottle. Many S&Ls simply went crazy. They forgot about their original mission of helping citizens save money and buy homes. Instead they were out to make money, just like full-fledged banks, only without the same regulations as banks.

An avalanche of bad business was about to be unleashed, and the tremor that started the landslide was the new freedom S&Ls now had to offer pretty much whatever rates they wanted to for certificates of deposit (CDs). They could offer high interest rates for these short-term deposits, which drew a great deal of money into their coffers. And that was the problem. The S&Ls had to put this expensive money into investments with higher returns than they were paying for it. Naturally, higher returns meant greater risk.

Making matters worse was another wrinkle in the plot: the deposit brokers. These financial agents were paid a fee to put their clients' cash into the highest-return CDs out there. In the heady days of the mid 1980s, when S&Ls were expanding wildly and hungry for cash, a deposit broker could extract favors from an S&L in exchange for deposits. The favor was usually to invest some of the funds into one of the broker's deals.

The most notorious example of deposit deal making was Michael Milken, a broker for Drexel Burnham Lambert, who herded funds to S&Ls in exchange for their investments in his junk bonds. But he was far from alone, and along with junk bonds came highflying, high-return real estate deals.

Interestingly enough, the S&Ls also raised money by taking their existing low-interest mortgage loans and selling them off at a discount to Wall Street firms. These firms then bundled the loans together and sold them as government-backed bonds—thanks to the mortgages being backed by Freddie Mac or Fannie Mae. Sound familiar? Ironically, the S&Ls themselves would buy these bonds, owning $150 billion of them by 1986.

And so began the great real estate boom of the 1980s, with S&Ls investing in real estate like mad. While some of the money went into single-family homes, a great deal of it went into large commercial projects, such as office buildings, shopping centers, apartment complexes, planned communities, condominiums, and so forth. Big loans were being made.

Everything looked good at first, as it usually does in a boom. The market was fueled not only by the pools of new capital, but also by years of economic growth—the so-called decade of greed, or the Reagan prosperity years, depending on your point of view. And just as U.S. real estate prices did from 2001 to 2006, real estate prices in the 1980s jumped to new heights.

Unfortunately, when prices reached these new heights, they ran smack into a market flooded with product, thanks to years of S&L-financed overbuilding. Naturally prices started to decline—as they do in any market where supply exceeds demand—and borrowers who were caught in the down draft began to default on their loans. A downward spiral began that would pull the S&Ls down with it and ultimately trip the country into a recession (see Figure 8.1).

The looming crisis was inherited by the administration of George Bush the First. His administration reacted by setting up something called the Resolution Trust Corporation, or RTC, in the summer of 1989. Its mission was to rescue the failing S&L industry,

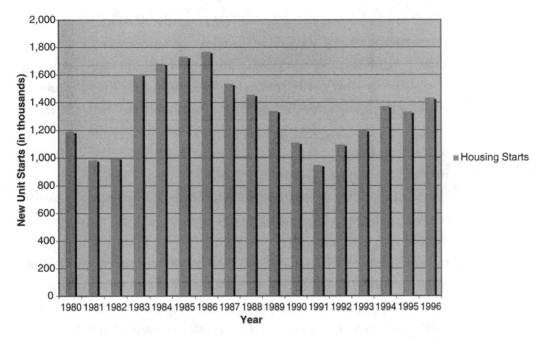

Figure 8.1   **The Housing Roller Coaster: U.S. Housing Starts, 1980–1996**

Source: U.S. Bureau of the Census

now saddled with a huge portfolio of overvalued junk bonds and hollow real estate assets. The RTC would shut down the S&Ls that were in trouble, make good on their losses, and sell them off to new and better managed groups.

It sounded like a good idea at the time, but the results were disastrous.

What happened was that regulators overreacted (what a surprise!). They went to the S&Ls, and to the mainstream banks as well, and told them they had too many real estate loans on their books. Basically, the regulators told them to get rid of these loans, to get them off their books, starting with the worst underperformers. They basically told the S&Ls to take back properties from borrowers who were in trouble.

Now, why would banks and S&Ls indiscriminately take back properties knowing they were going to lose money in the process? They would have been better off giving at least the more reputable borrowers an extra year or two so they could ride the market out, wait for things to stabilize, and then go about liquidating any assets they had to in an orderly fashion. Instead, they were pressured by federal bureaucrats who had no understanding of real estate markets.

Compounding the pressure to accelerate foreclosures, new federal regulations in 1989 also called for stricter capital requirements, demanding higher loan-loss reserves for S&Ls. These were designed to shore up the S&L industry, but instead created waves of discount sales, as S&Ls started dumping their portfolios to raise cash.

Making matters even worse, the regulators were also telling banks not to make any new real estate loans and not to extend any loans. Consequently, they were pressuring them to call in commercial loans, which are by definition short-term—one-, two-, and three-year—loans. This was a nightmare for commercial developers, who were suddenly unable to roll over their short-term loans. How could they? Existing loans that were in good standing were being called in, but regulators were at the same time telling banks not to make any new ones available. So, even projects that were not initially in bad shape found themselves in trouble, unable to raise capital.

The lack of new loans also dried up the pool of potential buyers. It was a double whammy. Regulators were forcing S&Ls to sell, while at the same time making it more difficult to find buyers, because nobody was making any loans.

And so government incompetence and interference in the market place made everything much worse. In essence, you had people making decisions who weren't competent to make them,

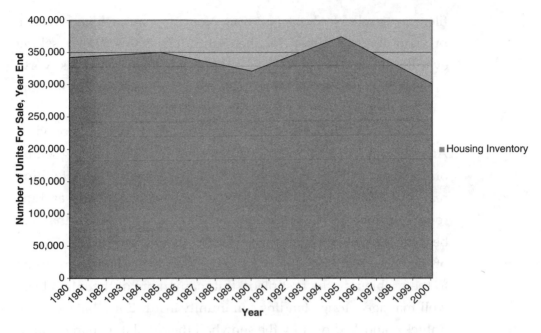

Figure 8.2   **New U.S. Housing Inventory, 1980–2000**

Source: U.S. Bureau of the Census

bureaucrats who had been not in the marketplace, but in government offices, for 15 to 20 years.

A vicious cycle had begun. More product was dumped on the market, which pushed prices lower, which led to more defaults and foreclosures, which depressed the value of S&L portfolios even further. (See Figure 8.2.) When an S&L's balance sheet looked bad enough, the regulators would come in, take it over, and then dump its real estate assets onto the market, further fanning the flames.

What happened was that the RTC became bloated with real estate, enormous portfolios of it. And rather than slowly feed this real estate into a market that was already oversupplied, the RTC instead flooded the market, selling it off at a fraction of true value. Their mandate, from the Oval Office right down to the rank and file, was to sell. Not hold. Not wait. Not ride it out, which is what a prudent investor would do. Their attitude was this: "We're selling everything, and we don't give a damn what we get. If it's worth $100 million, you know what? If the best we can get is $25 million, we're selling it."

Naturally, this further depressed real estate prices nationwide. Any S&Ls that had been simply shaky when the RTC starting selling off its booty in 1989 were soon sucked under by the tide of falling real estate prices. It was like a run on the banks and S&Ls, and the regulators just kept facilitating it. They were closing banks that had been healthy six months earlier, just closing them up. Yes, many of the S&Ls had been poorly managed, and that had contributed to the problem in the first place. But many more of them had been well-managed, long-standing community institutions that were just unlucky, knocked over by the snowball the regulators had created.

A lot of people were shocked at some of the institutions that were taken over, myself included. I'll never forget the takeover of the National Bank of Washington. At one point the stock had reached $25 a share. I remember sitting with some friends one day, talking about how the shares had fallen to $1, and what a tremendous opportunity it would be to buy a substantial position. I remember us all saying that the regulators would never close NBW, that it would be absurd; it was a well-run, conservative institution. Fortunately we never did buy in, because in the end the regulators did take it over. It was just that kind of environment; the market collapse swept the good along with the bad.

When it was all over—the RTC was dismantled in 1995—almost $150 billion in real estate assets had been sold off, the wreckage of somewhere between $300 billion and $400 billion in value created at the height of the 1980s real estate bubble. The debacle contributed heavily to the national recession of the early 1990s.

Could things have been different? Absolutely.

In the first place, the regulators should not have closed, en masse, the S&Ls and banks that got into trouble. They would have been far better off lending them money, or even giving them money, because it would have been less expensive to keep the banks open by allowing them to have additional capital.

Capital was the big issue. Regulators closed hundreds of otherwise healthy S&Ls because of insufficient capital, a condition often created by the regulators themselves. In essence, as the value of property went down, regulators told the banks to reserve capital for these losses, and when the banks didn't have the money to set aside as a reserve, the regulators closed them. That added more property to the market, lowering values further. It was a self-fulfilling prophecy.

What the regulators should have done was to keep the better-run of these institutions open. But the theory was that in order to protect the free market system, you had to go ahead and let these banks fail. Then apply the rules to them and close them, even if it cost the taxpayers tremendous amounts of money, which it did, because the federal government—using taxpayers' money—absorbed the losses.

The Real Winners

In the end, all of the real estate that was dumped on the market thanks to ill-advised federal agencies was absorbed. But it was not absorbed via the banking system.

When you had this flood of properties coming on the market, and no banks to make loans, and no liquidity in the banking system to buy, the private equity world swooped in. Basically, Wall Street and the private equity capital markets said, "Hey, wait a minute; there is a great opportunity here."

Say what you will. One thing about Wall Street is this: people on Wall Street can figure out how to make money under any circumstances. The day after somebody drops a nuclear bomb somewhere, these guys—along with the cockroaches—will be out there prospering.

What the Wall Street houses said was, since there is no liquidity in the market, we can go to our capital sources, we can go to our investors, and we can create real estate funds. Then we'll go out and buy these properties at fantastic discounts. And that's just what they did. Investment banks like Merrill Lynch, Lehman Brothers, Goldman Sachs, and Credit Suisse, and private equity buy-out firms like Blackstone and Donaldson, Lufkin & Jenrette, which had cash but were not regulated, bought up real estate at rock bottom prices, 25 cents to 50 cents on the dollar. The result was the creation (or you could say the transfer) of huge amounts of wealth, because not only did real estate values recover, they got better.

The people who had to give up their properties lost, while the people who bought didn't have to do anything except wait—wait for the markets to regain liquidity, wait for sanity to return. Because that's one thing about real estate: if you can hold on, if you have enough money to hold, real estate will bounce back.

A typical sale from this period was like the one that took place in September 1991, when GE Capital Corporation paid $527 million for $1.1 billion in troubled real estate loans on multifamily housing complexes in California, Arizona, Utah, and Colorado. By mid-decade these properties had all returned to their former values.

It really came down to who had cash. You didn't have to be a big investment house to benefit. There were some developers who could hold on to their real estate, and they didn't lose any money. And those who had capital were going to their banks and saying, "You know what, we want to buy our own loan back, but we'll pay you off at a discount." They were going to the bank and saying, "We owe you a million dollars, but we'll pay you $700,000." Or, "We owe you $100 million, and you know what? We'll pay you off in 30 days, but we want a 25 percent discount." So they were making money by going back to their own lenders and buying back their loans at a discount.

It was in the midst of this crisis, in the recessionary years of the early 1990s, that Bill Clinton became president of the United States. He had the great fortune of running during a time when the country had reached a point where it just wasn't going to take it anymore. It had gotten to where the American public was fed up with what the government was doing.

So when Clinton came in he dumped the bureaucrats and brought in advisors from Wall Street, in particular from Goldman Sachs and from Blackstone, two of the firms that had reaped huge benefits from the real estate crisis. Robert Rubin, a cochairman and 26-year veteran of Goldman, was first made head of Clinton's National Economic Council, and then Secretary of the Treasury. Roger Altman, who had joined the Blackstone Group as vice chairman in 1987, became Deputy Secretary of the U.S. Treasury.

So you had these two guys come to Washington after making a few hundred million dollars on Wall Street. They were basically saying, "We know this real estate crisis from the inside, and now that we have made enough money from it, we can show the country how to get out of it." And that's what they did. They said, "Wait a minute, we just need to calm things down." And once things calmed down, the economy started turning around, and values recovered.

On the Street in D.C.

While all this was happening I was living and working in the nation's capital, and it was here that I made a great deal of money in the down real estate market of the early 1990s. It was in Washington that I bought the site for my first hotel, along with numerous office buildings. I still retain ownership in the hotel, but ended up selling most of the buildings I bought in less than half a decade for three, four, and five times what I paid for them.

You could say that I was lucky to have been where I was at that particular time. Luck certainly had something to do with it. In the end, however, luck means nothing if you are not in a position to take advantage of it, or are not willing to seize the opportunity.

In my case, I was in a positive cash flow position when the opportunities arose to buy real estate at rock-bottom prices. I owned a local tax appeals business at the time, so when property prices started to drop across the country—and Washington was no exception—I was flush with clients; as you might imagine, there were scores of property owners who felt their taxes should be lowered to reflect the new valuations.

These clients did deserve a tax break, by the way, because prices across the city were plummeting. Similar to other metropolitan areas, especially in the Northeast and Mid-Atlantic states, the Washington market was exposed to an overbuilding of commercial space. They had what we called "see-through" buildings, where the buildings were empty—brand new buildings with no tenant build outs, so you could see through entire floors, window to window.

Buying in downtown D.C. was a simple decision for me. It was, in fact, one of the easiest business decisions I ever made. I knew that we were in the capital of the greatest, most powerful country in the world, and that no matter how far prices fell the market would eventually get better. People were going to keep coming to Washington; the government was going to keep getting bigger.

In the end I bought 11 buildings, beginning in 1992 with a bid that I placed on the historic Riggs Bank building at 900 F Street. The RTC was auctioning it off in August of that year, and I bid $5 million for it. Prior to its foreclosure, the property had a $15 million mortgage on it; I figured it was worth substantially more than my bid. There were some complications, including the fact that the current tenant—the University of the District of Columbia, which occupied the entire building—bought the former National Bank of Washington headquarters building (which abutted their main campus) from the RTC. Even the university wanted to get in on buying below value. Consequently, they no longer needed the space in the F street building, and vacated with almost three years remaining on their lease. Additionally the federal government didn't want to accept my low bid, but I eventually closed on the deal in 1994 and had negotiated a settlement with UDC for a 50-cents-on-the-dollar buyout of their lease. They delivered a check for $1,250,000 to me at closing. So upon my purchase I had immediately realized a cash profit of $1,250,000! A few years after closing I redeveloped the property into a Courtyard Marriott, which still generates substantial cash flow for me every month. In fact it is one of the top-performing Marriott Courtyard hotels in the world.

The other buildings I bought were mostly in that immediate neighborhood, the east end of downtown. These were purchased primarily from banks and private equity funds that had either taken back the property from their borrowers, or bought them in pools of mortgages for pennies on the dollar and foreclosed on the owners, and wanted to quickly resell them.

I bought several buildings on the 900 block of E Street, for example, from LNR, a subsidiary of the Lennar home building company. These were part of a package of loans that LNR had acquired from the FDIC. They wanted to monetize the loans and were looking for quick sales. That meant opportunities for savvy buyers who understood the inherent value of the neighborhood, people like myself. So I bought cheaply, leased out space cheaply to cover my costs, and held on for five years. What kind of profits did I make? I bought one E street property, for example, for $2.5 million in 1994. I sold it in 1999 for $10.5 million.

In other words, I was able to buy at 25 cents on the dollar. And because even these discounted prices were leveraged, my returns were not in the hundreds of percentage points but in the thousands. I made tens of millions of dollars just by doing nothing but waiting for the market to return. All I had to do was have the courage to go with my gut instinct, my knowledge about the local marketplace, and what common sense told me. Washington, D.C., was not going down the tubes, and I knew it.

Now, each deal was different, and each was its own story—though all have that trademark of being somewhat opportunistic, because that's where you find value. I bought one building at 60 Florida Avenue because it had belonged to a client of my tax appraisal business. It had been taken back by my client's lender, then the Maryland National Bank, later the Bank of America. So I was familiar with the property, understood its value, its tenants, and so forth. I paid $600,000 for it, and it cash-flowed immediately; in fact, I fully amortized the loan within three years. I later sold it for more than $2 million; not a killing, perhaps, but it was a property that carried itself, and I only put in $50,000 in cash.

Then there was the Peoples Drug Store warehouse site on New York and Florida Avenue, NE., a block away from 60 Florida

Avenue. It was a property I knew well, because my company also did the property tax appeal work for its previous owner as well as for Maryland National Bank after they took it back from my original client. At one point this property had been appraised for $26 million; when it was foreclosed, it had a $13 million loan outstanding. Now, with the recession in full tilt, and the neighborhood in disrepair, I was able to buy the building for $2.2 million; the bank even threw four single-family homes in with the deal. I sold it two years later for about $6 million. I got it so cheaply in part because it was an old warehouse and needed work. But it had development rights and excess development land, and I figured if I could buy a building for $2.2 million that had once been mortgaged at $13 million, it didn't have to move far back up the value chain for me to make money.

And so it went. Once people heard that I was assembling properties in the area they started approaching me: 910 F Street, for instance, came my way from the American Security Bank, which was subsequently closed. Either the bank or their broker called me because they had heard I was buying in the neighborhood; they had taken the property back and wanted to get it off their books. I paid $575,000 for it, and later sold it for $1,200,000; 912 F Street came my way in a similar fashion, from an estate that was being liquidated.

These deals were not too difficult, because I had sellers who were willing to sell. The opportunity was typically generated by a lender who had taken the property back and wanted to unload it. Since I was already on that block, the brokers or lenders naturally started calling me.

Of course, some of the deals took coaxing and courting. I remember one guy who owned 916 F Street. He had this kind of novelty store in the building, and he was kind of a wacky guy. He used to visit the property often and would tie a rope with diamond shaped flags across the front of his building. He would tie it to my building next door, and I would have to go down and nicely ask him to keep it on his building only—since I didn't want to piss him off. He also had a big ego, and for him selling the building was the big deal of his life, so he wanted to show me how good he was at negotiating. It took a while, but eventually he agreed to sell it for a price that made sense for both of us.

It wasn't the lowest price I paid. What the owner did not know, however, was that another nearby property was attempting to convert to all commercial but had a residential housing requirement to satisfy. The developer needed my new property to offload his residential requirement so that he could go totally commercial on his. It was a clear case of unlocking the value of both properties, and it turned into a win for both of us.

In most cases, however, it wasn't a matter of creatively unlocking value. In the case of downtown Washington, prices were lower than they had been in 20 years. To some extent, the same thing was happening in markets all over the country. In order for any given deal to be a bad deal, the market would have had to never recover. In order for it to be a good deal, all you had to do was hold on, because at some point the market would bounce back. If I had had more money at the time, I would have bought even more.

This is the opportunity of a down market, and this is the opportunity that presents itself to investors across the nation right now.

CHAPTER 9

Fundamental Values: Buying in the Right Regions, Cities, and Neighborhoods

A big aspect of the current real estate crisis is that it's indiscriminant. It's hurting every market in the country, even places with solid fundamentals. And that's where to buy.

I know it's redundant to repeat the old real estate adage about place—that where you buy is more important than what you buy—but it's inevitable. So I apologize ahead of time. But the slogan "location, location, location" continues to hold up today just as it has for decades and decades. It was what I was taught from the start: It's generally better to buy the smallest house in a wealthy neighborhood than to buy the biggest house in a poor neighborhood.

This is especially relevant when it comes to looking for value in the current real estate maelstrom. In certain places there has been wild, speculative overbuilding—Florida, California, and Arizona immediately come to mind—and local markets have not been able to absorb the supply. Certain cities, as well, stand out: places like Miami, San Diego, Phoenix, Las Vegas, and Washington, D.C., to name a few.

In most major U.S. metropolitan areas, however, there was not gross overbuilding. There was some overbuilding, and some gross overspeculation, to be sure, as prices were driven to unrealistic altitudes. But one of the characteristics of the current credit crisis is that it has been indiscriminant. It is penalizing and hurting almost every real estate market in the country, regardless of the particular excesses in any given community.

This is very different from the S&L/real estate collapse of the 1980s, by the way, which did not happen all at once across the nation. That debacle began in fitful stages and moved in regional waves, hitting some states much harder than others. It really began in Texas, when the spigot on the oil boom years of the early 1980s abruptly turned off in mid-decade. Texas real estate started to slide—prices would fall 25 percent—and with it a slew of Texas S&Ls. Soon neighboring states were infected, including Arizona, Utah, and Colorado. Eventually it spread to New England, Florida, and finally, despite heroic efforts to prop things up, California. Certain states, such as Ohio—where the governor preemptively cleaned up the S&L industry in 1985—went relatively unscathed, except by the overall national recession.

Compare that to today's environment, where, with the exception of a few stellar cities, the effects of the real estate meltdown are being felt just about everywhere.

Why the mortgage crisis of 2007–2008 has been so universal is a consequence of another of its unique characteristics: A great deal of it is driven by perception. I have heard more than one pundit observe that the media has been among the great drivers of potential recession in 2008. As television, Internet, and print media herald how everyone is defaulting on their mortgages, how the economy is heading downward, how credit is impossible to come by, and how important it is for people to hold onto their cash and prepare for bad times to come, the behaviorism of everybody from the average consumer to top bankers begins to echo these reports. People spend less, banks lend less, and everyone suffers together.

From our point of view, the extent to which the current crisis is driven by perception means it is an opportunity in disguise, a lucky break for those who are prepared to seize the day. This is especially true for people who are able to buy in regions, cities and neighborhoods where the fundamentals remain strong.

The fact of the matter is that people are still going to need to live and work in cities such as Las Vegas, Washington, D.C., New York, San Francisco, Atlanta, and so forth. In markets where there are strong fundamentals, the current mortgage crisis is a true buying opportunity.

What do I mean by fundamentals? These are the underlying determinants of economic stability and expansion for any metropolitan area, and they include such things as good job growth, sustainable incomes, sustainable industries, good school systems, strong tourism, good quality of life, and so forth. One reason that I feel confident about investing in a project in Las Vegas, for example, is that job growth in 2006 was the fastest in the nation—about 35 percent. Even with the economy sputtering in 2007, jobs continued to grow at 4 to 5 percent. The same was true of population growth, as 7,000 new residents moved to Las Vegas Valley each month.

Now, in 2008, Las Vegas is faced with the aftermath of a building spree that created too much supply. The housing markets in both Vegas and Reno have peaked, and there is a substantial decline in both prices and sales.

Does this mean that you should avoid buying in the Vegas market? On the contrary, there now exist opportunities that will certainly disappear once the housing supply returns to normal levels. You should buy there because the fundamentals for Las Vegas—taxable revenues, gaming income, and visitor volumes—are still rising, albeit at a slower pace than in 2006. This is in stark contrast to the national fundamentals of overall spending and income, which have fallen. Jobs in Las Vegas in 2008 have continued to expand at a higher percentage than for the United States as a whole. Nevada is also one of only seven states that does not impose a personal income tax, an impact that is magnified because it is located next door to the highest taxed state in America, the great state of California. (Additionally, Nevada is considered the state with the lowest probability of natural disasters!)

These are what I mean by fundamentals, and they are often unique to individual cities. Information on fundamentals is available to anyone willing to research a given city or area. In the case of Las Vegas, statistics are available through The Center for Business and Economic Research at the University of Nevada, for example. Other cities have similar resources, as does the federal government—via the Bureau of Labor Statistics, for example—and national data banks like city-data.com.

In the case of New York City, the fundamentals are extraordinary. It is a thriving city that hits all the go buttons: a strong employment base (Wall Street jobs make up 5 percent of all jobs in the city), sustainable incomes, powerful industries, excellent schools (New York University, Columbia), a potent tourism industry, a rich cultural life, and so forth. So it was no surprise then that in 2007, despite the real estate meltdown sweeping the rest of the nation, the average price for an apartment in Manhattan rose to a record $1.4 million in the fourth quarter, up 17.6 percent from the fourth quarter of 2006.

Granted, this number peaked because so many wealthy buyers bought so many exorbitantly priced condos. And economists are predicting 2008 price drops in at least some neighborhoods around the city. Nonetheless, key indices remain strong. In the fourth quarter of 2007, for example, there were 605 foreclosures in New York City. While that represented an increase of 71 percent over the same period in 2006 (354 foreclosures), as a percentage of New York's 3 million households, it was tiny when compared to other cities—0.02 percent in New York vs. 0.21 percent in Los Angeles and 0.25 percent in Miami.

Other figures defied the national downtrend as well, including the number of apartment sales in the fourth quarter of 2007, which climbed 3.2 percent compared to a year earlier. Apartments also sold 18 days faster than they did a year earlier, while the inventory of apartments for sale dropped 13.5 percent.

The point here is that cities with good fundamentals have suffered less than cities with poor fundamentals, or cities that went through more torrid expansions of supply. A quick comparison of housing price changes between February 2007 and February 2008 illustrates this point perfectly. According to the S&P/Case-Shiller Index, home prices in Detroit fell 16.5 percent from February

2007 to February 2008. This should be no surprise in view of the poor condition of the auto industry that is based in and around that city. Likewise, prices in San Diego—which has few major corporations headquartered there and was overbuilt because of its attractive lifestyle—also fell 19 percent.

Compare those drops to a city like Chicago, which has a highly diversified economy and is home to a platinum collection of major corporations, including Boeing, Sears, Walgreen's, Motorola, Caterpillar, and McDonald's. There prices slipped by a relatively modest 8.4 percent. Or how about Seattle, which is not only home to companies such as Microsoft, Starbucks, Washington Mutual, Amazon.com, and Nordstrom, but also did not see a speculative burst of building? There, home prices fell a scant 2.7 percent between February 2007 and February 2008. (By comparison, a composite of the top 20 U.S. cities showed a drop of 12.7 percent.)

The key is to look to cities where the fundamentals are strong, because these are the cities that will hold value. In such places, finding a good deal is better than finding a good deal in a city with weak fundamentals, because the recovery time is going to be faster in the stronger cities. What good will it do you to buy a $200,000 house in Detroit, even if it was once selling for $300,000, if it's going to take 10 or 15 years to return to its former value?

The fact is that people are still going to want and/or need to live and work in places such as Washington, D.C., New York City, the Bay Area of San Francisco, Los Angeles, Chicago, Atlanta, and so forth. The same cannot be said for many of the less vibrant cities in the rust belt, or in the South, or in the Plains States. So you need to look at the major metropolitan markets where people are more likely to live and work, and where there's always going to be a strong demand.

Again, each of these cities will have a different spread of fundamentals, and you have to consider these unique elements when looking at the viability of any given market. New York and Chicago are both corporate powerhouses for publicly traded companies, for example, with strong financial service industries as well. The Bay Area of San Francisco is strong because it is a melting pot for new technology, situated near Silicon Valley, and has a growing job base. Los Angeles is a good bet, thanks to an amazingly diversified economy, with manufacturing, entertainment, and tourism, not to mention its strong trade links with the world's fastest growing economy, China.

There are other less thorough ways to pick markets that have the best chances for a quick recovery. Rather than search the deeper fundamentals, you can compare a few simple indicators like job growth, foreclosure rates, and inventory. Good job growth, low foreclosure rates, and bloated inventories make good candidates, for example, since these factors indicate strong fundamentals combined with opportunities for bargain prices. Using this kind of radar leads to cities as diverse as Salt Lake City, Raleigh, Orlando, and Houston.

I myself am from Washington, D.C., and I have always done well there with investments. I have felt it to be a safe bet in down times because of the presence of the federal government. Regardless of the endless promises by politicians to shrink government spending, the odds are that government will continue to grow, and with it the surrounding economy. Also, we have a change of administration about to take place, and that means a lot of new people will be coming in, no matter who wins, and they will be looking for housing. Additionally, the region has become a fertile ground for the IT industry, with companies such as America Online, as well as many entrepreneurial spin-offs from government-sponsored R&D efforts. So that market is essentially as close to being recession-proof as you can get.

Looking at Washington, D.C., and my investments there, brings up another important point: neighborhoods.

People are creatures of habit. People like the same location, the same community. It's not by accident that people continue to live in certain places for many years and that housing values are historic in nature; neighborhoods shift slowly in value and tend to retain value in historical context.

This is often a matter of perception, in terms of how people look at certain areas, but these perceptions tend to hold up over time. Usually it takes a catastrophic event to radically change neighborhood values. Miami Beach, for example, has done well for a long time, and will continue to do well. It had a nasty downdraft, however, when it was hit by the Marielito boat lift, when tens of thousands of poor Cuban immigrants and ex-criminals moved into the area in the early 1980s. But that was an external circumstance, and it's unusual for someone (in this case Fidel Castro) to throw 125,000 people out of their country and send them to Miami. Knowing this made a lot of people rich when the Art Deco District and South Beach came back to life in the decade following that boatlift.

The key to buying well in this environment is to look first at cities and regions where there are good market fundamentals, and then at neighborhoods within them. These will also follow certain market fundamentals, such as good school systems, quality environments, access to recreation, proximity to culture, and so forth, but regardless of the underpinnings they can all be tracked historically through the information sources we've previously discussed. At www.realtor.com, for instance, you'll learn that neighborhood quality was the most important factor for buyers in 2006 and that the majority of buyers who viewed homes online then drove by the house; so much for virtual realty. At www.trulia.com, average prices, median prices, and prices per square foot are all broken down over time by individual neighborhoods in the major metropolitan areas.

What you want to find is a significant price retreat in the best neighborhoods and in the more stable neighborhoods. This distinction is important, by the way. If you are investing in high-income homes, then you are looking at the best neighborhoods. If you are investing in middle-income housing, then you are looking for the stable areas. What you might find is that prices in the best neighborhoods don't pull back as much, because wealthy people can continue to afford to buy, even in a down market. Also there is usually a limited supply, because there are fewer people in that price range. So, if you look in the better (but not necessarily the best) neighborhoods in the stronger cities, and if there has been a significant retreat in value, and if there is an opportunity that presents itself, then this is the place to buy.

In my own case, I followed this geographical paradigm in my Washington, D.C., purchases that we looked at in the last chapter. Not only was I convinced that Washington would rebound from the banking crisis of the late 1980s and early 1990s, I chose a neighborhood—the east end of downtown—that had historic precedent as a thriving commercial corridor. I bet that it would return to its former greatness, and I was proven correct.

Then you have situations in which the overall fundamentals of a city may not be strong, but particular circumstances make it an attractive investment. Places like Miami, for example.

Miami had suffered a real estate drought before the last boom; when it was finally unleashed, however, the overbuilding created a flood that could not be absorbed. It was like a huge rainstorm in the desert where the sand can't absorb the water quickly enough. What you had in Miami was a flash flood. But, just as with a real flood, over time the ground will absorb the water—and the market will absorb the excess housing. Even cities that were overbuilt will recover, as long as demand returns.

What happened in Miami was a combination of things, including an open-door policy by the city government, with no height restrictions. Across Biscayne Bay, in Miami Beach, there was a moratorium on high-rise construction and a generally antidevelopment government and constituency. But Miami had virtually no holds barred. With the promise of quick returns, a wave of condo construction was driven by investors—local, national, and vacation-property buyers.

Then a few things happened. The immigration laws were changed, limiting visas to the United States and making it more difficult for foreign nationals who wanted to buy. At the same time there were suddenly 60,000 units coming online, putting downward pressure on prices, and therefore making units less attractive to speculators. Vacation buyers, too, started to shy away, revealing a fundamental weakness in the market, which is a lack of underlying demand by local residents. Miami is not a job-generating community; to the extent that it is, the jobs are in the service industry, and not high paying enough to afford $700 dollars a square foot for an apartment, or $700,000 for a 1,000-square-foot condo. It's just not that kind of market.

Now, does that mean there are no buying opportunities? Absolutely not. If values go down 30, 40, or 50 percent, there's a time to buy there too, because ultimately national and international buyers are still going to find Miami attractive. It still has no state income tax, it still has a great climate, it still has a culturally and ethnically diverse environment, and it's still a fun place to have a vacation home—as well as being close to the Eastern Seaboard and to Latin America and the Caribbean. In the end, although it may take longer, Miami will recover. European investors in particular will eventually look at the low prices and the currency exchange rates and see the great big bargain; that's part of what will bring things back.

They say that what goes up must come down. In real estate, what goes down generally comes back up. It's just a matter of timing, and that depends on picking the right geographic locations based on the underlying fundamentals of a given region, a given city, and a given neighborhood. Just make sure to do your homework first.

CHAPTER 10

Specific Observations: Making the Deals

Once you understand current values—where
to buy and when to buy—you still have to make
that perfect deal. So size up your seller.

One of the things I have always espoused in my career as a real estate entrepreneur is that you make your money on the way in, not on the way out. That means that you make your money when you buy property, not when you sell it.

This sounds absurd on the face of it, of course, since you don't realize any profits until you actually cash out of any deal. What I am saying is simply that the quality of any investment, and its profit potential, is based on buying at a good price. If you buy at a price that is well below value, you have already made your profit.

119

This sort of buying usually takes place in a down market, when other people are not buying and lots of people want to sell. Then prices are reduced to make a sale happen, and you as the buyer have leverage. Now, you can always make money in a rising market, so long as prices continue to rise. But in such cases you make money only by selling at a premium price. The differential between your buying price and your selling price is based on a rising market, on valuations yet to occur. This is what I mean by making your money on the way out.

Making your money on the way in means that you have purchased at a price point that builds in the differential, the distance between the price you paid and the price where you know you can sell. In a declining market you can find opportunities to purchase properties below their replacement costs. Generally, properties sell for more than their replacement costs; this is especially true in a rising market where there are a lot of newly constructed homes (the simple theory here is that there needs to be a profit for the builder, similar to producing any product for sale). Still, these kinds of below-value purchases can occur in all kinds of markets.

In the summer of 2007, for example, just as housing values collapsed across Michigan, a company called Northern Michigan Land Brokers purchased 7,300 acres in the northern part of the state known as the Upper Peninsula. The price they paid was $7.3 million, or about $1,000 an acre. Despite the shrinking demand for both housing and land across the country, the purchase price of $1,000 an acre was a bargain, because Northern Land Brokers was able to sell it in smaller parcels for $2,000 an acre.

In this case, the buy was for 80 parcels bundled together, acquired from companies that owned the land for its timber value. What Michigan Land Brokers realized was that growing numbers of baby boomers from the region's metropolitan areas—including

Chicago, Detroit, and Grand Rapids—were interested in purchasing land for recreational and retirement purposes. You could say this was simply a case of buying at wholesale and selling at retail, a function of economy of scale. But what they really did was unlock the land's value, transforming it from logging tracts to prime pieces of wilderness, packaged for baby boomers hungry for a slice of nature. And they knew the value of this before making their buy.

So, a great deal of making money in real estate is to see value that others did not, and to unlock value where others could not. I have succeeded in many of my most lucrative deals by doing just this. My purchase of the Bath Club in Miami Beach, for example, was based on my ability to have the land rezoned for higher density. I was able to see the inherent value of the property, for which I paid $10 million, if its potential could be realized. I was able to do that, and eventually earned a profit of nearly $60 million once the property was fully redeveloped as an oceanfront, mid-rise luxury condominium project, along with four oceanfront mansions. (The irony here is that if I had just sold the site a few years after the rezoning I could have made almost as much. This was due to initially purchasing the property below its then current value; creating additional value by rezoning the property to increase height and density; and then realizing the extra push from the rapidly rising market.)

I know this is a far cry from what most small investors are able to do, but the principles remain the same: Buy a quality property at a price below its value, and you have already succeeded. If you buy at a high price, you are at the mercy of the market.

Let's bring this down to specifics. In Chapter 4, we discussed where and how to find properties for sale. These sources included databases for multiple listings, namely the properties catalogued by the National Association of Realtors. In Chapter 11 we will look at where to find properties that have been foreclosed and are now for sale through HUD and other agencies. The other source is through personal contacts—from real estate professionals who are in the mix to bankers who are in charge of liquidating property. Word of mouth is a powerful medium, and I cannot tell you how many deals have come my way because somebody mentioned them to me. Then, once you find interesting properties, keep the information to yourself. Remember that old saying "loose lips sink ships"? It's very true. I have come across several opportunities because people were talking about deals they were working on; there generally was no productive business purpose for the discussion, and they were just showing off.

You can also find deals in your immediate environment, and by that I mean by just driving around and looking at the marketplace—say, in a neighborhood that you know has strong underlying value. You never know what you will come across, or how intuitive your understanding of value can become, just by being on the ground. In more formal terms we discussed in Chapter 5 the ways in which you can value property, be it through comparable sales, replacement costs, or the income approach. With this kind of information in hand, along with your informed intuition, it's possible to make a good choice when acquiring property.

These tools are just the jumping-off point, however, since the really spectacular deals are going to be based not just on the asking price, or the location and square footage, or on what you might do with the property, but on negotiating with the seller. It's one thing to find a property you want; the next critical step is getting a great deal on it, and for that you have to understand the seller's motivation.

People sell their property for different reasons. In the case of homes, some owners are people who want to trade up, and need to sell. Others may be relocating, and need to sell. Still others may be spec builders; they also need to sell. Otherwise selling is an elective, and not urgent.

After you find a property that fits the basic profile of a good deal—a good price in a good location—then look deeper. How long has a property been on the market? The longer the better, because that means the seller may have grown weary and be willing to take a lower price. How many times has the price been lowered? Again, this is a sign of seller motivation; the more times it has been lowered, and the shorter the interval between each drop, the higher the motivation. How many offers have they received? And why were they not accepted? Obviously, if no offers have been received, the seller is more anxious; however, if previous offers have been rejected, knowing why will give you further insight as to the seller's motivation. Some sellers can be very stubborn and will only sell if they get their price; on the other hand, they may not need the cash and may be willing to hold financing at below market rates or even take a second mortgage if their price is met, thus reducing your cash out of pocket.

Knowing as much as possible about the sellers themselves helps, too. Are they investors trying to flip the house? If so, a long time on the market is more painful for them than it is for owner-occupied homes. They may be willing to negotiate rather than continue to pay the carrying costs of insurance, mortgage, and taxes. Have the owners relocated elsewhere, or are they planning to? Again, these sellers are motivated to sell quickly rather than continue carrying the property and keeping it maintained.

Speaking of maintenance, a lot can also be learned from going to the site. Is the house occupied? Has it been maintained? If the house is unoccupied and in a state of disrepair, then the owner has probably lost interest in getting the highest possible price.

There are other categories of sellers worth examining as well, such as individual speculators with contracts on properties now worth less than their purchase price, or project developers with excess supply who may wish to sell at cost, which means below current market price. We will discuss these unique opportunities in Chapter 11, especially in regard to the condo market.

As for buying from builders with excess product, this generally falls into the category of new housing projects, developments that are typically sold off in multi-unit lots. We will also discuss this in Chapter 11 as well. The immediate focus, however, is on buying individual properties from individual owners, and how to get the best possible deals.

My own most recent experience in buying a home took place in Washington D.C., where I wanted to return after living in South Florida for many years. Granted, I was looking at very high-end housing, but the principles involved are universal.

I was house hunting in August and September 2007, the worst part of the mortgage crisis to date—though things would get worse, as it turned out. I was hoping to buy a house in Massachusetts Avenue Heights, one of the best neighborhoods in Washington, near the vice president's mansion and near all the embassies. Warren Buffett had a home in the neighborhood, as did Senator Bill Frist. In the end, I found a house I liked that had been on the market for an original price of $9.3 million, and I was able to buy it for $5.9 million, even though one next door had sold a month earlier for $8.4 million. That house was purchased by an investment banker from Goldman Sachs, and it was smaller than mine. But I was able to buy very, very low because I was paying cash, and I was willing to close immediately, within a week. But that wasn't the only reason.

For starters, I'd been making offers on other houses, so I was flexible. In other words, I wasn't emotionally attached to the house. As in all matters of business, you cannot become emotionally involved. When it comes to a home, this is especially true. People will always pay more if they become emotionally involved, and fall in love with a property. That is something you want as a seller, but not as a buyer.

I had other leverage with this particular house as well. The sellers had purchased it as a real estate investment. They bought the house in 2004 for $2.5 million, gutted it, and put another $2 million plus into renovation. So, they were into it for an amount that was relatively low compared to the asking price, but—and this is a big but—they were paying at least $30,000 a month to carry the property, maybe $40,000 a month. So this was eroding their profit, and since no one was living in the house, every month that passed meant more money lost. They might as well sell it for the first decent offer; after all, we were in a down market and they were in the business of selling. The sellers had also made at least two mistakes: they put the house on the market while the renovation was ongoing, thus it did not show well; and they cut corners when renovating, in terms of the level of finish. They did not even build out the closets. What this told me was that cash was tight and they were trying to conserve money; thus they were very motivated sellers

Another house on the market that I looked at was in the suburban neighborhood of McLean, Virginia. It was listed at $16 million, but I had gotten them to agree to sell it for $8.8 million. It was a brand new, 20,000 square foot house. The sellers had initially built the house for themselves and then changed their minds about moving in. Nonetheless, they finished it off and figured they could sell it and make money in the process. Well, the market went against them. And even though they were wealthy and didn't have to sell, they wanted to move on; a lot can happen to a 20,000-square-foot house that is sitting empty.

Another factor in the psychology of bidding on this house was an earlier attempt by the owners to auction it off. They held the auction in August, using a private auctioneer. Now, that's not a good time to sell in Washington, D.C. That's when Congress is in recess; it's hot and humid, and most people in the Washington metro area who can afford to leave are gone. It's the time when, years ago, I won the bidding process to buy the old Riggs Bank building on 900 F Street from the FDIC, which I later developed into a Marriott Courtyard hotel. I put in what I thought was a ridiculously low bid, but because only one other party was bidding, mine was the highest.

So the sellers in the case of this house made a terrible mistake in auctioning it in August. Even without the bad timing, by having an auction it showed me they were fed up. So I offered $7.75 million, which was below their reserve. They wanted $8.2 million plus a 10 percent buyer's premium, basically $9 million (they were offering me some credit, so it was actually $8.8 million). But this was for a $16 million house, which two years earlier could have fetched that price! They got hit by the down cycle, however, and just when they were ready to get rid of it. Also, the house was empty, with no furniture in it, and no effort to make it look nice. There was a leak in the ceiling from the air-conditioning overflow tray, so you could tell they weren't even spending the money to have someone routinely check on the house. They were clearly ready to move on.

I bid on another house in McLean, and found the same sort of willingness to radically lower the asking price. This one was on the market for $5.5 million (it was originally on for $7.5 million), but I eventually got them down to $4.2 million. In this case the family had moved to Florida for business reasons, so they figured they'd sell their house. No big deal except that the market went against them and the house was sitting empty. Meanwhile they were still paying the carrying costs. So I knew they wanted to get out and move on with their lives, and not have to worry about what was going to happen to the property.

What was interesting about this particular house was that it was not well maintained. It was dirty—and this was a very expensive house, with 17,000 square feet and 35 rooms. But it was a mess. They didn't even pack up all their clothes. The furniture was worn, the place needed painting inside and out, and the landscaping was not being kept up. Basically, the owners had decided to stop maintaining the home. What that told me, and what that would tell any investor, was that they were frustrated and tired of trying to sell it. Psychologically they had detached themselves from the house, and they were now looking to save money, because the carrying costs were getting to them.

The truth is that all of these houses were worth more than I had offered to pay. But the down real estate cycle and the uncertainty about the future, combined with the fact that I was willing to close immediately, allowed me to put in a low bid that was accepted. Even with the times being less than optimal for sellers, each of these situations had an added opportunistic element.

I also needed a place to live, since I had intended to relocate to Washington, and that is one of the great parts of residential real estate investing—you have to live somewhere anyway.

So I had the opportunity to buy well, spend a few hundred thousand dollars finishing the house properly, then live in it, knowing that I could sell it again at anytime and make a profit. Not only would such houses return to their former values, they'd get a normal appreciation of at least 10 percent a year, adding to my profit. In the case of the house I ended up buying, the one for $5.9 million on Mass Avenue Heights, I can foresee that house returning to a value of $9 million when the current mortgage crisis is a thing of the past. So I will make $3 million on the deal.

Though Washington, D.C., is a city that has strong fundamental values, as we discussed in Chapter 9, it is no different from anywhere else where the markets favor the buyer. I did the same sort of thing in Santa Fe a few years earlier. The Santa Fe luxury housing market had never fully recovered from the downturn of the 1990s, and sales activity was relatively slow. Few people were buying luxury houses at that time, and the area was in a slight real estate downturn. I bought a house from the bank for $2.3 million, used it for two years with my family, got some great vacations and memories out of it, then put it on the market and sold it in two months for $2.9 million. Not a killing, mind you, but certainly a house that paid for itself. The bank that sold it to my wife Katrina and me agreed to hold 95 percent financing at 4 percent fixed for 30 years plus a credit for a few inspection issues. As a result we were able to buy the house with $190,000 out of pocket, so we tripled our money in two years.

The lesson here, again, is that the investor or potential buyer should not just look at the asking price for a house that's on the market, but for telltale signs of seller motivation. In the case of the Santa Fe bank, the motivation was built in; banks are not in the real estate business, and generally want to get foreclosed properties off of their books. They will also be creative in their efforts to sell.

Once you can sense when a seller is motivated, then you can start identifying the more opportunistic situations. That's what you want to look for, opportunistic situations, signs of opportunities being present. And those kinds of insights will lead you to the best deals.

Another advantage is that in a down market the future is murky. This is a good thing for buyers—the perception that the immediate future is unknown. People don't know how bad it's going to get. They are afraid—like the real estate speculators who agreed to sell their $9.3 million house for $5.9 million. They were concerned that, if they let me go, when would the next person come along? Would it be two months? Would it be six months? Would it be a year? This is another reason you can buy well in a down cycle, and that's when you make the money.

Now, all of the above examples were about sellers who had the ability to lose money. The investors who built the house on Mass Avenue Heights were breaking even, at best, but they considered themselves lucky to move on and live to fight another day. The couple that built the house that listed for $16 million was probably going to lose a few hundred thousand dollars, but they could afford it, and at least the ordeal was over. The family that moved to Florida from the house in McLean would also lose some money, but for them, also, getting out from under was a relief. These were situations where the owners could afford to take a loss.

The situation with the average house, in the midlevel housing markets, is different. Here, the challenge is whom you're buying from. These individual sellers can't afford to lose money and therefore can't slash prices as readily. Now, if there are increasing numbers of foreclosures, you will have opportunities to buy midmarket homes from banks at steep discounts, something we'll discuss next. But many of the midlevel properties with apparently motivated sellers—owners who took on exotic loans and are having problems making the payments—won't necessarily drop their prices.

Think about it. These people can't afford to sell at down-market values because they owe too much. They borrowed 90 percent, 95 percent, even 100 percent of the sale price, and they borrowed to buy a $300,000 house that is now worth $250,000. But they can't sell to you at $250,000, because they would then have to write another check to the bank. So there is little opportunity there for negotiating until the bank comes in and takes it back—or unless the bank has offered the owner an opportunity for a short sale, in which the bank agrees to take less than what is owed, for the sake of getting a bad loan off their books.

You also have to consider that this is an election year and that numerous seats are up for grabs in both the Senate and the House. Congress is going to have to do something to help alleviate the nation's mortgage problems. Already in early 2008, Fannie Mae and Freddie Mac—the government-sponsored agencies that guarantee mortgages for banks—were allowed to lift their ceiling on single-family home mortgages as part of the national economic stimulus package. Whereas conforming loans were previously maxed out at $417,000, Fannie and Freddie could, until the end of 2008, guarantee so-called jumbo-conforming loans of up to $729,750 in cities with high housing prices.

The point is that many distressed homeowners are trying to hang on pending new programs that might help them refinance or sell at a better price. They are waiting to see what programs the local, state, and national governments are going to come up with to alleviate the mortgage crisis before they let go of their properties. So, the best place to go in your community to buy an individual house for a discount, based on a troubled mortgage situation, is to your local bank or mortgage company.

These banks will have an REO (Real Estate Owned) department or officer, and their job is to manage the disposal of property that has been taken back by the institution. Their job is to get rid of this property quickly. You need to establish a relationship with this department or officer; sometimes this can be done through a real estate broker who has a good connection, while at other times you can do so directly. In either case, you have to be in a position to act quickly, with excellent credit and ready cash, as I did in Santa Fe. Otherwise you will lack the credibility needed for this relationship.

In the meantime opportunities to buy from motivated sellers will be there, and you should be on the lookout for indications. You'll always have situations where people have relocated, or where speculative investors are tired of carrying properties, or where a property is being sold to wrap up an estate proceeding, and so forth. Such circumstances will present opportunities.

Keep in mind also that when you are bidding to buy a house from an individual seller or a bank, once you do the inspection, and it reveals deficiencies, you get a chance to renegotiate the price again. Naturally, your advantage in such cases is based on what deficiencies show up in the inspection. Little nit-picking items, like paint needed on the door trims or a door knob not working, will not get you much of a reduction. But a potential roof issue, a potential heating issue, a potential hot water heater issue—these give you the right to terminate the contract and the power to ask for a lower price. You can also use the inspection period to lock down your financing.

Of course, the best tactic may simply be the art and act of being disciplined and waiting until you find the right deal. The important thing here is self-control. Set your target price and don't cross it. If the deal doesn't meet your criteria, move on to the next one, because there is going to be another opportunity coming. It's like running after the subway or bus. You miss one, and the next one comes along a few minutes later. It's just down the road.

The key is buying well. You are going to have to look at many different properties to find that buy—you've got to kiss a lot of frogs to find a prince, as they say—but eventually you will find your perfect deal. The signs are there if you have the patience to see them.

CHAPTER 11

Techniques, Tactics, and Tricks: Useful Tools to Make Money

Understanding real estate principles is vital, but it also helps to know a few things about auctions, foreclosures, bank-owned properties, and contracts for preconstruction sales. In other words, how can you best leverage cash and credit, or just one of the two?

Having understood that a down market offers tremendous opportunities for you as a buyer, and having understood where to buy, and from whom to buy, there are still some practical things you need to know that can help you when it comes down to the seminal event itself, the actual purchase. Some of these tools may also influence your decision on when, where, and what to buy, since they open further avenues of opportunity.

The best way to look at the kinds of tools available to you today begins with your particular situation; from there we can look at some unique opportunities that have more to do with the sellers' situations. But let's start with you.

There are really just two variables when it comes to homebuyers: cash and credit. There are those with cash and those without. And there are those with credit and those without. Mathematically this produces four configurations: people who are flush with both cash and good credit; people with limited cash but good credit; people with some cash but no credit; and finally people with neither cash nor credit. Let's just say that as we descend in this list, the creativity factor has to rise proportionately.

The best place to be as a buyer will never change, and that is to have both capital and credit. In a down market, it gives you the high ground, the position of advantage. In the closing years of the 2000s, it is highly unlikely that banks and mortgage companies will make the same sort of exotic loans they did in the first half of the decade, such as mortgages that financed up to 100 percent of the purchase price. The trend is in the opposite direction, especially in troubled areas and especially with banks, the institutions that are stepping up as Wall Street–backed mortgages evaporate. Banks have already increased the buyer's required equity participation, that is, the down payment. Conditions will vary from bank to bank, and from mortgage broker to mortgage broker, but whereas 5 percent and 10 percent down was once acceptable, mortgage lenders now require 15, 20, or even 25 percent down. And that means, generally speaking, you need cash.

Now, if you are in a position to pay entirely in cash and close quickly, your power to extract a good deal is spectacular. It reminds me a little bit of how boxing promoter Don King used to entice

Mohammad Ali to take on one of his title matches, including the Rumble in the Jungle in Zaire. Other promoters might offer Ali a bigger purse for a match, but King would show up with a brief case full of cash. It may have been only $50,000 or $100,000—I say only because that pales in comparison with the multimillion dollar purses being offered—but the sight of the cash, the instant gratification, usually swayed Ali to pick King's offer.

The same is true when it comes to buying property. If you can offer the seller cash—which means no delays, no qualifications, a quick close in a matter of days versus weeks or months—then you can ask for, and often get, hefty discounts. When I bought my home in Washington in 2007, the seller reduced his price by more than 30 percent, and a lot of that had to do with the fact that I could close in a matter of days by writing a check. (Even if you are borrowing some of the money from a bank, a big down payment will save you money in the form of a better rate, as we discussed in Chapter 7.)

Extracting a discount because you are in a strong cash position isn't limited to individual investors, of course. The way in which private equity funds made a killing in the early 1990s, as we talked about in Chapter 8, was based on the same principle writ large; it is true whether you are a major investor on Wall Street or an individual, small investor.

The mortgage meltdown of 2007–2008 is no exception. Despite the fact that the Wall Street investment banking firms had huge write-downs—they were the ones who repackaged and invested in subprime mortgage securities in the first place—hasn't stopped them from taking advantage of buying opportunities in the down times. In December 2007, for example, Morgan Stanley bought a portfolio of 11,000 properties from troubled homebuilder Lennar

Corp. for $525 million. The properties were previously valued at $1.3 billion, so Morgan Stanley got a 60 percent discount for their cash deal.

Auctions

There is also another venue where cash, as well as good credit, rules the day: the world of auctions.

There are basically three kinds of property auctions: those held by professional auction houses, those conducted by the government, and those executed by foreclosure attorneys for banks. There are lots of variations in actual practice—estate liquidations, land auctions, county municipal auctions, federal auctions—but it really comes down to these three categories.

Professional auction houses sell residential and commercial property at the behest of their owners. These properties have typically been on the market for a long time, and the sellers are tired of carrying them. Successful auctions can speed up the sales process, and sometimes the fever of bidding can jack up the price. In addition to speeding up the sales cycle, owners hope to leverage the auction house's web of connections with real estate agents, bankers, developers, builders, investors, and so forth. These type of auctions also bring a sense of finality to the sales process.

The government auctions are held either by county governments or by the federal government. On a county level, the properties—more often than not vacant parcels of land—have been foreclosed in lieu of property tax payments. On the federal level, the property has been seized because of criminal activity on the part of the owner; usually it's the failure to pay income taxes or the filing of bankruptcy by the owner. These can be substantial properties, even high-end luxury real estate.

Bank auctions are straightforward: After foreclosing on a house that has fallen behind on payments, the bank will auction the house off, hoping to cover the outstanding balance that is owed the bank, along with the legal fees for the foreclosing attorney.

Professional auctions are typically held on the premises of the property up for sale; they may be held at a public venue when multiple properties are on the block. Bidders have to register with the auctioneer's office and post a certified or cashier's check for a percentage of the estimated value of the property, typically 10 percent. If you're not the successful bidder, this money is returned. If you are the successful bidder it goes toward the purchase price, and you proceed to a closing (if your deposit turns out to be less than 10 percent of the amount you bid, you will have to make up the difference right then with a personal check).

Closings take place in 30 to 45 days from an auction. If you are unable to get the financing you need to complete the closing—or are unable to close for any reason whatsoever—then the deposit money you put down at the auction is forfeit.

There are two ways real estate is sold at such auctions, either via "absolute auction" or "reserve auction." In the absolute case, the property will be sold to the highest bidder, regardless of top price offered. In the reserve case, the seller has the right to reject the top bid for the property, based on a minimum price he or she has in mind. There is also a "minimum bid auction," which is similar to a reserve auction except that the minimum acceptable bid is published. In this case the bidding will start at this price; no offer below is acceptable, and the best offer above wins. It's sort of a hybrid of reserve and absolute.

There are a few other things to keep in mind at professional auctions—a buyer's premium will be tacked on to your winning bid, for example—but the most important thing is that the properties are sold "as is." You cannot withdraw at a later time because of problems with the property. So the first rule for buying at auction is to have the property professionally inspected before you bid. The auction house will offer a schedule of preview dates so that you can examine the property ahead of time.

Government auctions work in a similar way. First there are the county auctions, typically conducted weekly or monthly by the office of the county tax collector. These include low- to moderate-income housing that has been seized due to unpaid property taxes; more typically it is a plot of vacant land. Lists of these properties are available prior to the auction and can be inspected during normal business hours at the offices of the county tax collector, the county assessor, or even at county public libraries. Some counties make them available online, and some charge a fee for this service.

As for deposits and minimum bids, these vary from county to county, and from state to state. Usually the minimum bid is what it will take to pay the outstanding taxes on the property in question. Deposits can vary. Los Angeles County, for example, requires a $5,000 deposit prior to the auction. Miami–Dade County requires a cashier's check only after the auction has been held, in an amount equal to at least 10 percent of the winning bid (you may have to carry several smaller checks, but—and confirm this with the clerk's office—you should be able to make these checks out to yourself, then endorse them at the auction. This way, unused checks can be redeposited in your account.)

The other aspects of the county auction process are similar to the professional auction houses: you should inspect before you buy if you can, because everything is sold as is; you have a stipulated period of time to close, after which your deposit is forfeit; the auctions are held out loud, and require you to be present; anyone can attend.

County auctions are one arena where cash is king, because what is sold is usually a derelict piece of property with no immediate income potential and little chance of being financed. If you scroll through county sales records, you can see that the sale prices are usually quite modest, rarely exceeding more than a few thousand dollars, because the local government simply wants to get the delinquent tax bill paid.

Then there are the federal auctions, which involve homes, buildings, and raw land seized by the feds, usually for income tax evasion or bankruptcy as we said, but sometimes for more nefarious crimes. These properties tend to be larger and more expensive than those sold for back property taxes, and far fewer are up for sale. These auctions are handled by the U.S. Treasury Department; their web site at www.treas.gov/auctions/treasury/rp shows the latest homes coming up for sale around the country.

These properties are sold primarily via on-site verbal auctions, or at nearby properties scheduled for sale the same day, although online auctions are held as well. While there is no minimum bid there are reserves (not revealed prior to sale), and the auctioneer will announce at the time that the final bid is "subject to the acceptance of the seller" if it did not meet the reserve.

The general public is welcome at the on-site auctions. You have to bring a photo ID and a cashier's check for down payment, the amount of which is listed in each property's Terms of Sale, as well as submit an application that you download from the web site. If you don't make the winning bid you keep your cashier's check. If you do win the bid the check is your deposit, and you will forfeit that deposit if you fail to close for any reason. As with all auctions, sales are as is.

The federal sales web site for housing (www.homesales.gov) includes not only the houses about to be auctioned by the Treasury Department, but also a much larger selection of HUD properties, listed by city. These are the foreclosed properties that we discussed in Chapter 6, backed by FHA and VA loan guarantees then turned over to HUD by the lenders. Some are up for auction, but most are part of HUD's inventory of homes that were not successfully sold at auction. All properties listed will accept bids, but they must be submitted via a HUD-registered broker. All of these houses come with prices but are open to lower offers; they also show the amount you can borrow for repairs, assuming you are making an FHA loan for the financing.

The third category of auction is the bank auction, conducted by foreclosure attorneys to liquidate properties that banks have foreclosed. These auctions are similar to professional and government auctions in many ways. They are open to the public, they require a cashier's check from the winning bidder (the amount can be stipulated by the attorney ahead of time, or they can require 10 percent of the winning bid), they sell property as is, closing is required within a certain period of time or you lose your deposit, and so forth.

The variations and details are as follows. Most bank auctions are held on the steps of the county courthouse, just as they were a century ago (habits die hard) but may also be held at the office of the foreclosing attorney, at the property, or at some designated public place. These are "minimum bid" properties, with the starting bid set at the amount owed to the bank plus any attorney fees.

One big difference about bank auctions is that the properties you are bidding for may still be occupied. Banks cannot evict the homeowners before the actual foreclosure auction. Once you own the property, therefore, it may become your job to evict. Now, most occupants will move voluntarily, but in cases where the property is not vacant, you must be prepared to use the sheriff's office to help you evict—or else factor in some sort of cost of doing business, such as paying moving expenses for the former homeowners. Additionally, these properties are generally difficult to inspect before you purchase them, and so your bid must be more conservative.

At bank auctions you must also be aware of the first and second trusts, that is, first and second mortgages on the house, as well as any liens. If the house is being auctioned to satisfy the first trust, no problem. Any amounts greater than the payoff to the first trust go to pay the second trust, then to any liens; if the amount doesn't cover the next-in-lines, too bad, because all trusts and judgments against the property are wiped out by the foreclosure auction. Now, if the auction is for the second trust, watch out; the first trust still has to be paid off. Actually, it has to be paid off first, regardless, which is why second mortgage lenders rarely push a house into foreclosure unless they are confident the bank auction will cover both the first and second trusts.

The final thing to watch out for at bank auctions is IRS liens. You can ask the foreclosure attorney if one exists, or you can find out through the court records. These must be paid; if not, the IRS has a 120-day "right of redemption period" during which it can take back the property from the new owner. Now, you will get the money back you paid at auction (repairs or improvements are lost), but you've wasted your time and resources on a property that produced nothing for you.

Overall, regardless of the kind of auction, the basic rule is never to buy a property that you have not seen yourself. A lot of auctions sell property in distant locations, either houses or land. They can seem like a great bargain; they usually are not. So a good policy is to believe nothing and to check everything yourself. This may or may not include actually having the property professionally inspected, but least make sure it appears to be in good shape, and then research comparable prices in the neighborhood. Remember that auctions are final, and they offer no recourse if problems later arise.

Another iron rule is to decide ahead of time what your top price is and to stick to it. This is a matter of discipline. There is always another deal waiting around the next bend, so don't become emotional about a given piece of property. You want to make your money when you buy, and that means the right price; if the bidding takes it past that, then it's some other person's problem.

The best place to find out about auctions is to check your local newspapers, since all auctions must be posted for general public notice. Next you can get information from your county government; sometimes this information is posted online, sometimes you have to go to the courthouse (you need to look where civil cases are posted for the bank auctions), and sometimes you need to visit your county tax collector's office (for local government auctions). For federal auctions you can check the government web sites. You can also consult with your real estate agent.

Another source is to subscribe to one of the many online foreclosure listing services (use the search term "foreclosure listings"), which amalgamate many of these sources for a fee, usually about $40 per month. Most offer free trial periods, but beware the fine print that locks in your credit card.

One of the more popular of such sites is realtytrac.com, which is linked into Microsoft, and uses their Virtual Earth satellite photo system to give you a bird's eye view of properties for sale. They list new homes for sale and some for-sale-by-owner properties—along with leads for mortgage information, and so forth—but they specialize in foreclosure data, sorting properties by county. The site basically tracks each property through the foreclosure process, and lists according to:

Preforeclosures—identifying properties when the filing takes place.

Foreclosure Auctions—announcing time and place of the auction.

Bank Owned Foreclosures—the properties that are taken back by banks because no one bid the minimum price at auction.

In the end there is virtually nothing on these sites that you can't dig up yourself from public records; what you are really paying for is convenience, being able to check out everything quickly, and the chance of coming across something you missed. The data available in online foreclosure listings should include what the last owner paid to buy the property, the current assessed value for taxes, how much is owed the lender, and when and where it's set for auction. But you should still check out everything yourself, and you'll have to do legwork no matter what. In their section on Bank Owned Foreclosures, for example, realtytrac.com gives little more than the institution's name; you will have to track down the phone number and someone to speak to, unless you want to avail yourself of the site's Contact Agent button.

Buying from the Bank

Speaking of bank owned foreclosures, this is something else you need to know about. When banks foreclose on houses and put them up for auction, the minimum bid is typically a combination of what is owed to the bank and what will presumably be owed to the foreclosing attorney. Now, if there is little or no equity in the house, or more is owed on the property than it's worth in the marketplace (commonplace in today's exotic loan environment), then no one will bid that minimum. No one may even show up at the auction.

In such cases the property is taken back by the bank and it becomes what is known as an REO, the acronym for Real Estate Owned by the bank. If the property had a VA or FHA guarantee, then the property goes to HUD, and the bank is reimbursed for its loan. But if it was a conventional loan, without VA or FHA backing, the property joins the bank's REO portfolio of bad loans. The bank assigns a senior manager to dispose of these properties. This is whom you contact.

Remember, when you buy at auction, you've got to have cash on hand to step up and buy, often without any professional inspections. You need 10 percent at the auction and typically have 30 days to close, so that adds to the risk if your credit is weak. It creates opportunity for the person who is in good financial condition and who has some very strong credit. Even if all you have is cash (and terrible credit), you can still acquire the property at auction and flip it to another investor before you have to come up with the financing to close.

If, on the other hand, you have adequate credit to borrow, sometimes the better opportunity is for you to wait for the foreclosure to happen and the property to go back to the lender. You then go and buy from the lender directly, on a negotiated basis, as opposed to buying at auction. It is certainly a less pressured environment.

You can find out about REOs by calling the REO manager at any number of banks. If you are interested in a particular piece of property, you can call the foreclosing attorney after the scheduled auction date to see if it was taken back by the bank. Your real estate agent can also find out about REOs, which are listed in the MLS as foreclosures or bank-owned properties.

When you find an REO that interests you, your assessment of value follows the same assessment it would for any property. The advantage of buying an REO is that the bank is highly motivated to get the properties off of their books, and that opens the door to substantial discounts.

Why does the bank want to shed these properties? First, to clean up their books; these properties represent bad or nonperforming loans, and are liabilities, not assets. Secondly, banks are not in the real estate business and are not prepared to manage or maintain housing. The longer they hold these properties, the higher their carrying costs, and the greater the chance for damage or deterioration.

How can you get a good deal? You can leverage several things in the negotiating process, as we discussed in Chapter 7, including knowledge of how much give there is behind the asking price. Was the property covered by Private Mortgage Insurance (PMI)? This is required from homeowners by many banks when the down payment is less than 20 percent. Whatever the PMI payoff was, you can figure the bank will go that much less on the price. Another advantage to press is when property is out of state; a local bank is more likely to take a lower bid on real estate they cannot oversee.

Other things to look for are similar to those we discussed relative to seller motivation in Chapter 10. How long has the property been back in the hands of the bank? The longer the time, the more motivated the bank will be to sell. How expensive are the carrying costs? The higher the costs for taxes, insurance, homeowner's fees, and so forth, the more motivated the bank. Is the property being maintained? If the place is deteriorating rapidly, the bank will be more anxious to sell.

One other opportunity available when purchasing REOs is that the lender may be willing to provide financing. When my wife

Katrina and I purchased our vacation home in Santa Fe, New Mexico, it was an REO. The property was a spec home by a luxury builder that was originally projected to sell for $3.5 million. The market was soft, however; the builder became overextended and was foreclosed. The lender put it back on the market, and in August of 2005 we purchased it for approximately $2.2 million—with the lender providing 90 percent financing at an interest rate of 4 percent fixed for 30 years, plus the right of one assumption from a future buyer. We sold the property in August of 2007 for approximately $2.9 million, and the new buyer assumed the loan.

Credit versus Cash

Now, to return to our paradigm, auctions for property are great if you have the cash going in plus the credit to close on financing. If you have cash but no credit, then auctions can offer some low-end land or low-income property that you can purchase outright. Even if you don't have enough cash for an outright purchase, having some goes a long way to mitigate bad credit. As we discussed in Chapter 7, lenders respond to cash; even with a miserable credit score, lenders will still lend if you put down a high enough percentage of the sale price. They will do so because the cash mitigates their risk, assuaging them as much as a good credit score.

Now, supposing you are on the opposite side of the equation, with good credit but no cash? Everyone has seen the ads for real estate strategies you can execute with no money down, and most people are skeptical. But you shouldn't entirely discount this possibility. Ultimately, the classic tale of rags to riches in America is a no-money-down story most of the time. I built my first high-rise office building, at 2100 Martin Luther King Avenue in Washington,

D.C., without a dime of my own money. The only way to get rich when you're not is to do it with no money down.

When it comes to buying real estate, good credit can make up for a lack of cash; the better your credit, the lower the amount you need to put down. If you are fortunate enough to live in a part of the country where housing prices are not exorbitant—let's say Glendale, Arizona, rather than Boca Raton, Florida—and you can buy at a price that comes under the FHA cap, then a good job and good credit can get you in for a tiny percentage down, as low as 3 percent. Surely you can raise $7,500 towards a $250,000 house from friends, relatives, savings accounts, 401Ks, garage sales, and salary advances.

What if you want a conventional loan or even a jumbo loan, and don't have all of the 15 or 20 percent deposit, but still have that shining credit report? There is one other alternative: taking back a note from the seller. This is just what it sounds like: the seller becomes the lender, and takes back a promissory note that you pay just as if you were paying a bank or mortgage company. Sometimes a seller will give you a note for all or most of the selling price, especially if they can get a good return.

A note like this is rare, however, since it means the seller cannot pay off their own loans on the property, plus it puts the seller in the position of having to repossess the property if you falter in payments. And the less the equity involved on the buyer's part, the riskier it seems for the seller. Still, there are circumstances where the seller will take back such a note, and in these situations what makes the risk tolerable is your stellar credit. And, just like when it comes to making a low-ball offer, it never hurts to ask.

Take my house on Broad Branch Road in Washington, for instance. I bought it with my wife in 1991, and it turned out to be one of our most spectacular homes, a 13,000-square foot mansion on 2.5 acres where we later held a fundraiser for Bill Clinton on his way to the White House. How we bought it was almost as spectacular.

We happened to be driving on our way to look at some antiques when we passed the house and saw a FOR SALE sign. I had known that house since I was a boy: a handsome Tudor-style home on Rock Creek Park. But the price they wanted—$2.5 million—was too much for us. We took a look at the house anyway, and we made an offer for $1.4 million, with 90 percent financing by the seller. And guess what? They took it!

A big reason they took that offer was, I admit, unique to the situation, just as the house was unique. A powerful local architect had it built in 1929 as a gift for his daughter on her wedding. She lived in it all her life, and when she passed away it was to be liquidated as part of the estate; when we made our offer it was the last asset left for disposal, so selling it would let them close out the estate. I knew this because I had asked the broker how motivated the seller was.

Another reason they accepted the offer was that the house was sitting empty, in a down market, and they didn't want to have to pay the property taxes, insurance, and other ongoing maintenance expenses. But the kicker was that we had impeccable credit, so we looked like a good risk. Also, we were paying them a higher interest rate than they could earn in a bank money market account; thus it was actually a good investment for the estate that produced monthly cash flow for the descendents. We never missed a payment with them, either, and when we sold the property in 1996—for $2.75 million—the new owner, with the estate's consent, assumed the note.

Now, as I said, it will take the right circumstances for a seller to take back most of a property's value in a note. A more likely alternative is to borrow most of the purchase price from the bank and have the seller take back a note for the balance.

This is far more palatable for most sellers because the risk is significantly mitigated. Say you are buying a single-family home. The people have owned the home for a long time, they want to retire in Florida, and they don't need all the cash right away. Also the house is almost paid off, so they have built up considerable equity. Let's say you get an 80 percent mortgage from your lender. That gives the owners more than enough to pay off their remaining debt, with plenty of cash to spare. So they agree to hold a second mortgage for the remaining 20 percent.

This is just what I did when I bought my mother's apartment back in 1990. I paid $125,000 for it. I got a 90 percent mortgage, then I got the seller to take back 10 percent in seller financing. So I did it with no money down, and when interest rates came down a few years later I refinanced the apartment and paid off the seller.

These days, banks are not so keen on such arrangements; VA and FHA loans generally require the down payment to come from the borrower's funds, and conventional lenders will more than likely want to see the 20 percent down payment in cash (though for some this is not a problem, especially if you have great credit). In such circumstances where the bank wants to see cash, you may have to close using borrowed money, with a separate commitment from the seller that, postclosing, they will refund the down payment and hold a second mortgage for that amount. This is how you buy properties with no money down.

Good credit offers you one other tool that is helpful, especially when you have little cash: the prequalification letter. This is the equivalent of getting a line of credit. It means going to a bank ahead of time and getting a commitment from them for a certain amount of financing, based on your income and credit rating. Not only does this allow you to bid for any house with confidence, it also gives you an edge when negotiating with REO managers at other banks. Prequalifying for an FHA loan gives you similar leverage for less expensive properties.

A prequalification letter is not only like having a line of credit; it also means that you can close quickly, which is one of the advantages of cash when it comes to negotiating with a seller. If they know they can make a quick sale—that you are ready to go, thanks to that prequalification letter from the bank—they are far more likely to accept a lower bid. When you don't have a lot of cash, a prequalification letter is like having a blank check for up to the qualifying limit.

The final condition of our paradigm is when you possess neither credit nor cash. This is a tough corner to be in when it comes to taking advantage of the down real estate market, because in the end you cannot acquire real estate without one or the other.

You do have one option, however—literally. For those with no cash and no credit, you can still obtain a lease with an option to buy, thereby creating a window of time during which you can rebuild your savings and credit rating.

In a red-hot market, this is rarely an option, since sellers can find buyers with relative ease. In a down market, buyers are scarcer, and there are going to be lots of people with properties they can't sell. From these sellers—owners whose properties are sitting empty and idle—you can sometimes rent with an option to purchase.

In such scenarios, you are going to have to offer a purchase price that is higher than what the cash price would be today. If this represents a good deal for the seller, he or she may be willing to lock in that price for a period of one or two years, during which time you are helping him or her carry the property by paying rent. Or, maybe you take a one-year lease with a right to renew for a second year, with one option price for year one, and a second option price for year two. Or you could have a contract that escalates the purchase price every quarter or every six months, either at a predetermined rate or indexed against some benchmark, like inflation or the prime rate.

Not many sellers will agree to this, but some will, especially in communities where there is a big inventory of unsold homes and properties are sitting empty. During the option period, you can accumulate some savings, rebuild your credit, and then buy the property later. Just make sure the contract allows you to forgo the purchase without penalty. Then you will actually be playing the market, with an option to buy if prices go up, and the power to walk away if the market stagnates or falls.

Buying from Investors and Builders

Most of what we have discussed above can be employed in any real estate environment. A down real estate market, especially one with excessive inventory, presents other unique opportunities as well.

One sector that has fallen into trouble is the condominium market. As we saw in Chapter 2, the real estate meltdown of 2007–2008 has been caused in large measure by oversupply, too much product at once. Nowhere is this more painfully apparent than in the condo market, where presale buyers—especially speculators and second-home buyers—put down deposits for unbuilt units.

As these buildings approach completion, the buyers who contracted for units are now faced with the prospect of having to close. Many will walk away from their deposits, for different reasons. Buyers may not have the finances to close; in some cases they probably hadn't planned on closing, hoping to flip the unit before the closing date. With prices falling sharply in overbuilt markets, other buyers may simply not want to close on units that are worth less than the price their contracts call for.

This presents you with an opportunity: To go to these investors and say to them, "I'll give you half your deposit back, and I'll take over your contract and close." Supposing an investor put down $200,000 on a $1 million condo and is going to let his deposit go. Why wouldn't he or she accept $100,000 from you for the contract? It's certainly better than nothing, and you just saved $100,000 on the purchase price.

Once you own the contract on property, then you will be in the same position as the other investors who are holding paper on a purchase price that no longer makes sense. Prices have not panned out as expected, so they don't want to buy the unit.

Developers are for the most part happy to see you walk away; they get to keep the deposit, after all. These deposits vary in size, but 20 percent is not uncommon. This is a sizeable piece of change for the seller; if he resells the product at the same price, it amounts to a 20 percent bonus. Or the seller can then discount the unit by 20 percent to the next buyer, and still retain the same profit margin. So a seller is content to keep the deposit and not waste time or money in pursuit of the buyer.

Occasionally, very occasionally, a seller may try to come after the buyer, hoping a court will award him or her a judgment that will force the buyer to close. This is rare, however, since federal law in the United States typically limits the amount that a seller keeps to 15 percent of the price if the buyer balks. In some states, such as California, the rules are even more in favor of the buyer; no matter how much your deposit in any real estate transaction, the only thing that's at risk is 3 percent. You can put a $2 million condo under contract, and put down a $400,000 deposit, but you get it all back except for $60,000 (3 percent), even if you, as the purchaser, default.

So, generally speaking, if a buyer walks away from a contract for a condo or home, the seller is happy to simply keep the deposit. The main exception to this rule of thumb occurs if the buyer has signed a contract that gives the seller special powers to enforce the closing. This is why it's a good idea to have a lawyer review your contract, especially if it is for an expensive property.

More likely it is the contract holders—the buyers—who will sue the developers to get their money back, or to get a substantial reduction in the sales price, which is what you can do with a contract you acquire from a buyer who wants to walk.

The basis for these lawsuits are several but revolve around whether the developers have met the terms of their contract with you, some of which are federal requirements. The biggest issue is whether they completed your unit on time. Generally speaking, developers who are selling undeveloped property are required to register with HUD, and this registration requires them to complete the building in a certain period of time, usually within two years. Another requirement is that the developer issue property reports to each buyer, and get a signed receipt for them. These reports disclose extensive information about the property, including overall plans and contract requirements, and deviating from these can be grounds for a lawsuit.

Now, developers can get an exemption from the HUD requirements if they are developing a property of less than 100 units. So if you are buying in a project with less than 100 units, you have fewer options legally, because of such exemptions. Then you are relying strictly on the individual contract you signed with the developer, rather than on federal legal requirements.

Nonetheless, if you can find places where the developer has either violated HUD guidelines or your particular contract, you can sue to get your deposit back, and possibly for damages above and beyond that.

While the aim of the suit may be simply to get back your deposit, I think the other thing you can get from developers today are concessions. First you look at the option of suing, then use that option to position yourself to go back to the developer and ask for a concession. One might be to lower the price of the unit. Another might be to get the developer to hold a second mortgage on the property. Or maybe you get a combination of renegotiated price and having the developer hold a second mortgage. Remember, the developer doesn't want your unit back, because there's no one else to sell it to right now. You're his best shot.

A lot of people don't think they should go back to the builder for a price reduction because they believe it's not fair, or they won't get it. Forget about this way of thinking; if the developer was in the buyer's position they would almost certainly try to renegotiate the price and terms. The average buyer doesn't understand that everything is negotiable. The builders are expecting it at this point, both condo developers and housing project builders. There are more and more defaults on preconstruction contracts, with people not closing on their units and suing the developers instead.

This applies to houses as well as condos. If you have a contract on a house being built by Lennar, Toll Brothers, or any other builder-developer, no matter what income level you are at—whether it's a $200,000 house or a $2 million house—go back and renegotiate. Tell them that your financial circumstances have changed, that *force majeure* has intervened, and that you're not closing. Look, a lot has happened in the last two years. A lot has happened in the last year. A lot has happened in the last 90 days.

Tell them that you're sorry, but that you are not going to be able to close under the present circumstances. They can give you your money back, or you can litigate, or they can renegotiate and do something that makes sense for everybody, maybe sell it to you for what it's worth today. The developer is going to be happy to get somebody to close, and you can get a great deal.

Let's walk through the deal we started with above. You're looking at a million dollar condo in downtown Miami, and there's a 20 percent, $200,000 deposit from the purchaser. You go to that person and say, "You know what? I'll take over your contract for $100,000." That's your first savings.

Then you go to the developer and you say, "I'm going to sue you, you're late, you didn't meet the construction schedule, you changed the condo documents, there were things in the contract that you didn't live up to," and so on . Or you can offer not to sue in consideration for a renegotiated price, because today the unit isn't worth a million, it's only worth $700,000. So you offer not to sue and to pay $700,000 instead. The developer is going to have to think real hard about doing it.

If he does, you just paid $600,000 for a million dollar condo. And who knows, maybe you got an even better deal; maybe the developer sells it to you for $650,000, not $700,000. Or maybe you offer $50,000 for the contract instead of $100,000. Or maybe the deposit was for 30 percent, because it was a foreign buyer, and you keep another $100,000. (In fact, in terms of finding such a deal, there are going to be specific opportunities to buy contracts from foreign investors who put money down on unbuilt condominiums in international cities like Miami, Washington, D.C., and San Francisco.)

Now, this gambit takes advantage of the preconstruction sales environment, and that's going to be a window of opportunity that stays open for just so long. Ultimately, many of these projects are going to fail, and then the lenders are going to take them over and auction them off. That's going to present an opportunity for multiple unit sales, and you are going to see bigger investors coming in and buying blocks of units.

For you as a small investor, the opportunity is to go directly to the developer or builder who has a lot of unsold units, and to negotiate to buy a unit from them at cost. The sellers in this case will range from the developers of single condominium high-rises to the national homebuilders that construct entire communities in one stroke. You may be surprised at what you can buy.

Just think about it. What happens when a company builds a house for $200,000 and expects to sell it for $300,000 but can't, not in today's market? You want to try to buy it from them at cost, or even a little below cost. If they paid $200,000 to build a house, and can get rid of it for $175,000 or $200,000 in the current environment, they are going to sell it. So that's where the opportunity is, and that can mean buying from a national builder, or from a local developer like the investors who sold me my house on Massachusetts Avenue Heights. Just like the national builders, they took their shot, they were unlucky, and they just wanted to move on. Yes, they didn't make any money this time, but they didn't lose much, so they could move on. You are going to see more of that.

What's important to understand in these cases is what the property is worth. If the value has gone down from the time it was put under contract by, let's say, 25 percent, then the buyers are going to want to either walk away or sue the builder. Neither the buyer nor the builder wants to go through that. So there are going to be opportunities to take over the contract from the original buyer, and to renegotiate it with the builder/seller, or to go directly to the builder/seller to cut a deal. These can be win-win situations for everybody, where they avoid calamity and you get a great deal.

CHAPTER 12

Outside the Residential Box: Investing in Commercial Real Estate

The opportunities in real estate go beyond the residential marketplace; should you consider investing in commercial properties?

Although this book is not about megadeals or the art of becoming a developer, there are still plenty of opportunities to pursue in smaller commercial investments, and they are definitely worth considering.

Understanding commercial real estate is important because it opens up other options for the small investor. The supply and demand curves for commercial real estate often move in counter-vailing directions relative to residential markets. In other words, while one is going up, the other is going down, and vice versa. This is why larger developers, such as my company, often invest in multiple property types; this diversification can offset declines in other sectors.

Take our current mortgage crisis, which is largely due to the oversupply of residential product. Developers across the country were clamoring to develop residential, and the vast majority of developable land was being used for that purpose. Most developers did not want to build in the other market sectors—office, hospitality, warehousing—they only wanted to follow the soaring housing market. And as a result of reduced supply, these other sectors became much tighter and stronger. Ultimately, the smarter developers began to diversify their product type; some, such as my company, even began to diversify geographically. But it was classic herd mentality, and if you went against the herd and built a hotel or an office building during this time you made a fortune.

I found this to be true for a project we were developing on Brandon Street in San Francisco. We bought the property, a former industrial site that had become an office building for a dot.com company, and we were in the process of turning it into a luxury condominium. But the commercial market got so hot, thanks to a dearth of new product, that somebody came along and made us an offer to buy it for use as an office building, which it had already been. We sold the property for 60 percent more than we paid for it, in one year. The cash on cash return was several hundred percent, because we put down 10 percent and leveraged the rest. We paid $19.5 million and sold for $31.2 million, but we put in $1.2 million in cash, and made $7 million net.

As a small investor in commercial real estate, the size of your deal will probably be smaller than this, but the overarching principles are the same. It's all about how to create wealth through real estate. The specific rules of the game in commercial transactions, however, will change as you get into the nitty-gritty of it.

The current opportunity for the small investor that cannot be overlooked is residential rental properties. The residential rental market is getting stronger and stronger. People who are losing their homes are going to become renters, and even people who can afford to buy are renting, because they think that values are going to go down even lower; and, of course, those who can't afford to buy will rent.

A small investor can buy houses cheaply and then rent them out. When housing prices were high, it was difficult to rent them out at sufficient rates to cover the debt service and the operating expenses, which include taxes, repairs, and so forth. But now houses, and even condos, are getting to the point where you can buy them at a price where they make sense to rent out. Granted, the best approach is that if you need a home, then you buy one. But rental income carries your property until it appreciates. Then you can resell it.

In addition to single-family homes you need to look at the market for small apartment buildings, 4-unit and 6-unit buildings. Now is a good time to buy some of these properties as well. They will continue to hold their value as income-producing investments even after the mortgage crisis abates, because you are still going to have people entering the market every year—people graduating from college, or graduating from high school, and going into the job market. After a couple of years, these people will want to move on to a home, but for several years they will be prime candidates as apartment renters. Also, as we pointed out in Chapter 6, if you purchase a property with four or fewer units you will be eligible for FHA residential financing. You may even want to live in one unit and rent the other units out; this will likely enable you to live rent free. An additional benefit of owning rental properties is that much of the income is sheltered from income taxes and you will also receive other tax deductions. On the other hand, if you hold the property for more than one year and then sell it, your profit will likely be treated as a capital gain for federal income tax purposes.

So, the first logical step from buying condos and single-family homes is to purchase a multifamily property, typically a small apartment building with anywhere from four to 12 units. The question is this: If you are planning to buy a condo, and planning to live in that apartment anyway, are you better off buying a multiunit building, occupying one of those units and then owning the other ones?

A big part of the answer is tied to your personal circumstances and goals. Do you have the time to manage and maintain the building? It will eat up a lot of your weekends, but the results could be lucrative. Are you looking at making what amounts to a passive investment—waiting for value to return—or does your exit strategy include selling the building at a later time after you have converted it to condos? Again, that is a much larger time commitment.

Regardless, if you are going to buy an apartment building, you need to know a few things about being in the rental business.

One concept you should be familiar with is rent control, which refers to the various municipal ordinances that regulate the rent increases a landlord may legally enforce. It is by no means universal, but in cities such as San Francisco, Washington, D.C., and New York, rent control can have a profound effect on a landlord's ability to improve a rental property (if rent levels are controlled, it makes no sense to pay for substantial upgrades, for example).

The reasoning behind rent control is that it prevents excessive rent hikes that could force vulnerable, low-income families to leave an area. In effect, it is a tool for urban planning that helps sustain a balanced economy by making sure there is a supply of affordable housing. This, in turn, ensures a supply of workers for lower-paying service jobs.

In many cases the caps placed on rents only affect apartments that are occupied. In San Francisco, for example, landlords can rent out vacant apartments at market rates, but have to limit the hikes for occupied units to the national inflation index. Again, this is designed to bring stability to a community, to make sure that working-class families have adequate housing, and that there isn't an unusual amount of turmoil created by families forced to relocate.

Now, you can argue that rent control goes against the grain of the free market and can reduce not only the quality of housing (why make improvements you can't charge for?) but also the quantity (why make investments in new housing that you can't afford to rent?). On the other hand, you have situations such as the one that now faces the Florida Keys, where the high cost of housing has impacted the ability of hotels to find sufficient staff for low-paying positions.

Economic polemics aside, the point here is that you should check with local housing authorities or commercial real estate agents in any municipality where you wish to invest, just to make sure you understand the rent control ordinances that are in effect—if any. This will impact the economics of any plan to invest in commercial properties and will become part of the formula to decide whether an investment makes sense.

Working out a financial formula, by the way, should be a key ingredient in how you think about investing in commercial real estate. Among other things, you need to understand the economics of any deal before going to a bank for a commercial real estate loan.

When it comes to lending you money, a bank's criteria for commercial loans are different from those for residential loans. A residential loan relies primarily on the personal income level and creditworthiness of the individual making the application. A commercial loan is partly based on the creditworthiness of the applicant, but is mostly based on the building's ability to generate income and its underlying value. It is in fact the income generated by a property that has the greatest impact on its market value; so when appraising rental properties, the income approach becomes the most reliable indicator of value.

The question that banks want answered focuses on the business vitality of the property: Will the cash flow from the building be sufficient to service the debt? Is it already occupied, or are their prospective tenants likely to occupy? What about the creditworthiness of the present or prospective tenants, and/or the structure of the leases with those tenants?

Banks want to feel comfortable about what's called the income-to-debt ratio. By income, we mean the cash that is left over after all the operating expenses have been covered. What is left should exceed the mortgage and tax costs by at least 10 percent; banks would like to see the margin even higher, up to 30 percent. So the income to debt-service ratio (also commonly called "the debt coverage ratio") they are looking for is between 1.1 and 1.3. If you receive $50,000 in annual rent, and the operating costs are $30,000, then your net of $20,000 should exceed what you need to pay for the mortgage and the taxes by roughly $2,000 to $5,000. Banks may also want to see a reserve against future interest payments and repair costs, which would also come from this net. So you have to understand how the building you want to buy operates: what the day-to-day expenses are, how the rent compares to that, what the taxes are, and what the financing would cost.

As for your personal credit and income, these will still factor into the formula to some extent—banks typically don't want to lend to people who can't manage their own finances. But in the end, if a commercial loan goes bad, they are more interested in coming after the property than after you personally, and therefore they want to understand the value of the building, that is, its ability to generate cash. In other words, when a bank looks at a residential loan, it looks at your ability to service the debt. When it looks at a commercial loan, it looks at the property's ability to service the debt.

When it comes to your personal worthiness for a commercial loan, banks are not so much interested in breaking down your credit score as they are concerned about your integrity and your ability to manage. They would look, for example, at whether you had ever filed for bankruptcy or had any properties put into foreclosure. It's not impossible to get a loan with such black marks on your credit history, but it would be challenging. The bank's concerns could be overcome if you put together an investment team with creditworthy members. Or these concerns could be overcome by putting up more cash.

In the case of larger deals, it is most probable that the financing will be nonrecourse to the investor or owner; this means the property is owned by a limited partnership, limited liability company, or corporation, which in turn is owned by the investor/developer. In such cases repayment of the loan is guaranteed by the corporate entity but not by the actual investor/owner. In such instances, if the loan goes into default, the bank can only take the property back; they cannot go after the actual person who owns the property. This is how developers and investors who lose their properties live on to fight another day.

Cash always talks, by the way. If you put a substantial amount down in cash—let's say 30 percent or 40 percent of the value—then a lot of other deficiencies will be overlooked. The same is true if the building requires an investment for repair or upgrades. The bank wants to know where those dollars are coming from. If you have the cash, they are more likely to grant the loan.

Leveraging, Price, and Options

Having said that, the key to investing in income-producing properties is leverage. You want to put down the absolute lowest amount possible, and again it's the income generated by the property that helps determine the amount of debt you can have. For example, if the property's net operating income after real taxes and reserves are paid is $40,000, and the debt coverage ratio required by the lender is 1.15, then $35,000 is available for the payment of debt service—since $40,000 is about 15 percent more than the $35,000 needed (actually it's $40,250, but let's round off for the sake of argument). This income could therefore support an interest only-loan of $700,000 at 5 percent interest. Therefore if the property you are acquiring has a purchase price of $770,000, the income would support a 90 percent loan.

The other determining factor for the loan amount is the appraised value of the property; in this instance it would need to be equal to or greater than the purchase price of $770,000. Most conventional lenders would like to see a larger down payment than 10 percent, but there are some out there who would lend 90 percent, especially if you could get FHA backing. You can further leverage by getting the seller to provide a second mortgage or loan to the partnership (or whatever ownership entity you decide to use) that is not secured by the property. Some senior lenders (the holder of the first mortgage) prohibit second trust mortgages (since this complicates matters in the case of a foreclosure); in such cases the seller's loan would have to be secured by your interest in the ownership entity. This is a common practice with larger projects and will work with smaller ones.

There are, in fact, a number of values that you can bring to the table that will encourage banks to view your potential loan more favorably and increase your leverage. If you have a tenant in hand that trusts you to find a location for them, for example. You may not be financially strong, but your tenant is, and that translates into future cash flow. In my case, my first major commercial investment was tied to the tenant that I brought to the deal—the city of Washington, D.C. I had a commitment from the mayor to house city workers in the building I wanted to construct and needed to finance. It was a potent card to play. The result was that I secured 100 percent financing leverage.

There are other values you can bring as well: for example, a track record of having renovated or developed other buildings. This is unlikely in the case of a small investor who is new to the game; more likely the value you bring, in addition to cash, will be the creditworthiness of the tenants who are currently leasing or have preleased, or the stability of the property's occupancy levels. If these come across strongly not only can you get higher leverage but even lower financing rates as well.

One other thing to remember with commercial loans (other than FHA-insured loans) is that the free market prevails. There are few government regulations other than a cap on the maximum interest rate the bank can charge (to prevent what's called "usury"), and there are no Fannie Mae guidelines, just the bank's guidelines. Thus they are free to lend to you at a percentage point they believe to be appropriate. The federal government does have guidelines as to how commercial banks must govern themselves, but until there are problems within a bank the regulators allow them to use their own judgment when making loans.

Financing is one thing, of course, but the other thing is price—what you should pay for a property. Much more so than with residential property, the price of commercial property is tied to its future value, the expected future returns. If a building can be leased again in the future to better paying tenants, for example, or be converted from apartments to condos, then the seller will try to extract some of that future value in the form of an increase in the sale price. The seller wants to get paid now on that future value. So, while the loan for a building is tied to immediate cash flow, the sale price is more reflective of future value.

A good example of future value is a small office building in a strategic location. Its value may be tied to what is happening in the neighborhood and the likelihood that a large developer may want to acquire the building for future expansion. This was the case in my purchase of 916 F Street, which I discussed in Chapter 8. Its value was escalated by a developer who needed to use the building's residential capacity to satisfy housing requirements for an adjacent commercial property.

This, by the way, is the other side of the coin when it comes to future valuations. While such considerations may inflate the price, understanding these values yourself in a way the seller does not can result in a great purchase. This leads us to one of the great tools for hedging your risk while you unlock these values: options.

Let's say you find a downtown parking lot that is not zoned for much else. It has a limited value. But suppose you find out that the city plans to build a courthouse next door in a couple of years. If you can get the parking lot rezoned, it could dramatically increase in value as possible expansion space for the courthouse or as a development sight for an office building for lawyers, or even as a commercial building for stores catering to those who work in or visit the courthouse.

So you go to the parking lot owner, and offer him an option: you are willing to pay him $5,000 a month for the next two years, in exchange for an option to buy the lot at a higher price than he expects for it. He figures it's a win situation; either he gets a great price for the lot, or he gets $5,000 a month in free income. You also secure his approval to make a rezoning application to the local government. Meanwhile, you go through the rezoning process, and if successful you can now buy the lot at a fraction of its new value.

You may not even have to buy the property, but can assign the contract to a large developer who also sees the potential. In this case the developer is paying you some of the potential profit and then taking over your option to purchase and close on the lot. In order to do this, you will need to negotiate the right to assign your lease and option to buy when preparing the lease agreement with the property owner; but in so doing you haven't developed any building, just waded through the zoning process, and that requires a far smaller investment of time or money than developing!

A few other thoughts on options—if you are bidding for a property in a slow environment, you may be the only buyer, and the request for extended time from the seller should not be a problem. If you are in an environment that is more competitive, you may need to explain the situation to the seller. He will then understand why you are offering to pay $1.3 million in 18 months, rather than the $1 million he is asking for today, and he may be more inclined to give you the option. Just make sure you have the ability to walk away from the option without recourse, that is, without legal tie-ups.

Another thing to beware of in commercial real estate is the short-term rollover loan, which is common for large developers. The one thing about real estate is that if you can hold on through bad times the values will usually bounce back. So when you are doing commercial real estate deals, especially as a small investor, don't be so desperate to get the money that you'll accept a short-term loan or one where the lender can call it in if it feels insecure. Get a definitive term, and that will give you enough time to hold on in a difficult environment.

These concerns are by no means limited to you as a small investor, by the way. As we cycle through the current credit crisis, a few big names have gotten into trouble thanks to rollover loans that couldn't be rolled over. New York megadeveloper Harry Macklowe, for one, was unable in 2008 to refinance $5.8 billion in short-term loans he used to purchase a portfolio of commercial Manhattan skyscrapers from Equity Office Properties in early 2007. So they fell into the hands of lender Deutsche Bank. He also made the mistake of personally guarantying the junior mezzanine loan (the loan secured by his partnership interest) of approximately $1.25 billion, putting his other assets in jeopardy. He actually was forced to put some of his prized assets on the market (such as the General Motors Building on Fifth Avenue in New York City)to pay off this loan.

Finally, when it comes to getting a loan for the purchase of multifamily housing, if you start small—a 4-unit building—FHA will insure that mortgage for an individual so long as you occupy one of the units. If you can qualify for a FHA-insured loan, as we discussed in Chapter 6, then you will find it much easier to find a lender, and will have to put substantially less cash down.

This creates an entry-level opportunity in commercial real estate for just about anybody. You can start in low- to moderate-income housing, and you can qualify for that FHA mortgage with the income generated from the units; that cash flow can be part of the stated income you need to qualify for your loan from a commercial bank. Right now, for instance, you could go and get a four-family flat in Northeast Washington, in a low- to moderate-income neighborhood, and get an FHA loan. You as an individual could start out with just a decent government job, and then own this building. You just have to maintain the building yourself, do the painting on the weekend, do the upkeep, and so forth. And then you can build your real estate empire from there.

Beyond Housing

The other types of commercial investments you can make are for buildings that lease retail and office space. Remember that most retail outlets, including national brands such as Blockbuster or Starbucks, lease rather than own their space. And many of the buildings where they lease space are owned by small investors.

If this option interests you, your best tactic will be to look for a commercial building in your neighborhood, one that either already leases to, or has the potential to lease to, a small, community-oriented business. A building that is vacant or only partially leased with good future leasing potential is more desirable because you can create value by leasing the building and reap the economic rewards. Additionally, a building that needs renovation provides greater opportunity for profit as you will create value by completing the renovation. I would also say to look in your neighborhood, which emphasizes an important point: When it comes to commercial real estate, nothing beats being on the ground yourself.

Whether a given property will work as the retail location for a given business depends hugely on the neighborhood, even on the street itself. It is hard to understand the dynamics of a given location without understanding the neighborhood, its pedestrian and vehicular traffic flow, its retail needs, and its local population. Short of commissioning an expensive study on the demographics of the area, the best way to understand these dynamics is through your own personal, hands-on knowledge of a neighborhood.

If the property you want to buy does not have a tenant, by the way, this may prove to be an advantage; without cash flow the price will be reduced. Then, before you go for bank financing, you find a potential tenant. How do you do that? You hire a real estate agent, a commercial leasing broker, which is a very different animal from a Century 21 or a Merrill Lynch Realty broker. The business of a commercial broker is commercial leasing. To find a good one you may want to call some of your potential tenants and find out who represents them. You can also look to your chamber of commerce, or to your local board of realtors, for listings of commercial brokers. Then just ask around a bit. Get some references from the residential brokers you know, maybe somebody who sold you a house.

Although we are not currently in the same down market for office space as we are for residential housing, by the way, that is not true for retail space, which typically follows the housing market. Developers in the United States have, in fact, built more new retail space from 2005 to 2008 than any other commercial category. If consumer spending continues to fall, there could be some real bargains in the retail sector.

For retail properties—or for that matter office buildings or multifamily housing—the opportunity is that low prices mean you can cash flow the loan more easily. I've been asked how I could afford to buy so many commercial buildings in the slow market of Washington in the early and mid 1990s. I was able to do so because I bought them so cheaply that I was able to rent them out at reduced rates and still cover the debt service. With a down market, buying commercial property that you can rent is your best chance. When other people stop buying, they start renting.

The final kind of small commercial investment you should consider, if you are in a business that requires office space for yourself and your employees, is whether to buy instead of leasing your workspace. This can be either a small commercial building or an office condominium within a larger structure.

The advantages of buying your office space are several. First, it enables you to control your rent expenses in future years. If you own the office and are paying a fixed rate mortgage, this cost becomes predictable. If you are merely leasing, you could be subject to rent increases. Second, buying your space allows you to control it; any upgrades or modifications are yours to make, without landlord approval, and any investments you make in upgrades can pay off later if you sell the space. There are also tax deductions for depreciation.

The other consideration in buying your workspace is whether you want to participate in the office real estate market. Then you need to look at the space objectively as an investment, and apply general investment principles. What, for example, is the virtual cost of the investment—what else you could have done with the money—compared with the return? Say you bought a fixed-income CD instead. Would those returns outweigh the potential profit from your office condo? Would they outweigh your savings in rent along the way?

Whatever form your commercial investment takes, once you have found a property you are interested in, the final step—where the rubber meets the road—is the negotiation process. The two seminal events in real estate are the purchase and the sale, and how well you do with either depends on how well you can negotiate an attractive price. It's not that you won't make money if you are a bad negotiator. It's more a question of premium: people who aren't comfortable with negotiating pay retail, while those who are comfortable pay wholesale.

All of this, of course, is very entry-level commercial real estate investing. It's about the professional who buys his own space, or the apartment dweller who uses FHA to add some rentable units onto the deal, or the small investor who buys a small building for a community-oriented business. But this is how most real estate fortunes begin, with just that first purchase. It's the story of Tony Goldman, and how he went into SoHo in New York and bought one building, and then another. It's the story of Fred Trump, the father of the Donald, who got his start with FHA-insured multifamily housing.

What's to prevent someone from doing that today in Anacostia in Southeast Washington D.C., as I did in 1986? Or in the edgier parts of Oakland across the bay from San Francisco? Looking at what that community needs, making an initial commercial purchase, convincing a tenant to come in there—these can be based on your experience close to home, and that's probably the best way to start making such investments. Because if you are close to home you can make a decision based on what you know the community needs. And then bring it.

PART FOUR

SAVING YOUR BACON

(How to Avoid Getting Swept Under by the Subprime Tide)

_____

CHAPTER 13

Be Like the Rich: Change Your Way of Thinking

In America we have been conditioned to follow the rules. But what happens when the rules change and the system does not protect you?

One of the things that amazes me about this country is how conditioned everybody is to following the rules, and how much everyone believes in the powers that be. Rarely does the average citizen question the prerogatives, or the motives, of the large corporations that dictate so many of the ways in which we perceive the world. It is simply assumed that the large business interests know what's best, or at least have our best interests at heart. That, sadly, is rarely the case.

If we look at this phenomenon of misplaced trust in light of the credit crisis of 2007–2008, it is clear that many of the people who got into trouble with their mortgages trusted the market and the system and followed the so-called rules. Despite the fact that they are now in trouble, however, they are too embarrassed to fight back.

How should they act? They should act like the rich, and by that I mean they should think outside the box. Call it the Donald Trump rule of thumb. Trump lives in a multimillion dollar penthouse—and in several other such homes, actually—despite having filed bankruptcy twice on his casinos. He owns the Mar-a-Largo estate in Palm Beach, but doesn't pay his creditors. Think about that, living in an enormously expensive home, flying a private 727 jet, and not being able to pay your creditors. And yet banks still want to lend to him. If he can do that, why should you be embarrassed because you are overextended financially?

Part of what it takes to be rich—as well as to survive the current crisis—is to escape your programming of fear when it comes to dealing with institutions and to stop acting according to the rules of normal, average-Joe consumer behavior.

The first thing to do is let go of intimidation—in this case, of being afraid to negotiate with a big bank or lender. Again, if we look at Donald Trump, he actually had to give back some of his properties to his creditors, and put others into bankruptcy. Today he is nonetheless considered a huge success, his name synonymous with good business practices, despite some checkered deals in his past. So why should you have to act differently?

Trump is far from alone in his ability to reinvent himself and return to the game. Thanks to the real estate crisis of the early 1990s, there were quite a few successful developers who gave their property back to the banks, or who renegotiated their loans. These were some very high-profile people. Ian Bruce Eichner, for example, developed the ultra-luxury Continuum condo on Miami Beach. He essentially went bankrupt, but is now building another huge project in Las Vegas called the Cosmopolitan (though at press time he was gamely battling to fend off foreclosure in that overbuilt market). If he can do it—survive intense downfalls and then spring back—why can't you?

A big part of the answer is embarrassment. As consumers, people get embarrassed when they can't pay their bills. It's the way the system is designed, and it's nothing new; since the beginning of consumer spending, and especially since the days when credit was extended to the masses, the big companies have intimidated the average consumer.

The rich do not fall prey to this. They think they are beyond the average person's way of being treated, and in many ways they are. But it's not the money that makes them so, as much as their way of thinking. In the chicken or the egg conundrum, thinking outside the box is one of the things that made the rich rich, rather than the other way around. They have no problem telling a bank to bug off.

Now that I have succeeded in becoming a successful real estate developer—or rather in spite of it—I am still faced with what amounts to bullying by bankers. I currently have a hotel project in Marathon Key, which is one of the major islands among the Florida Keys that connect Miami to Key West. I have a construction loan from a bank, but I haven't been drawing it down because I don't have any presales. I am waiting for the market to improve before I commence development. Nonetheless, the bank wants me to add another million dollars in interest reserve because we did not commence construction. Given the *force majeure* of the market decline for condominiums in South Florida, who in their right mind would build a new project? We are in fact considering developing a luxury hotel on the site.

What I've told them is that we are facing a national crisis in real estate and that I'm not putting another dime in right now. If they want it back, then take it. Of course I'm going to sue them if they do, because what happened is that my lender, Freemont Investment and Loan, got into trouble due to the subprime mortgage crises. The FDIC came in and made them sell parts of their business. So they sold their commercial loan business to a Wall Street firm.

In essence, I had a deal with my original bank; they would have given me more money if we ran behind schedule. They told me not to worry about it. Well, I told the new lenders, "You guys are telling me something different, so I guess we are going to have to litigate over it. But I'm not giving you another dime, not one. Why would I? If I'm going to lose money in the deal, then I'm going to lose it now. And if I'm going to have to fight, let's fight now."

The lesson here is that you can't be too polite to fight. I have enough money in the bank to write checks all day long, but I'm not going to do so just to avoid upsetting a lender. Most people have the money to cover their obligations. But sometimes you have to say no, especially if you feel the situation is unfair, and that means not being afraid.

The problem is that we've been conditioned in America to be a part of the system and to follow the rules. We avoid confrontation. But the system is what's thrown people into financial calamity. The system is what allowed—even encouraged—the investment bankers on Wall Street to create exotic loan packages as a way to generate income. The reason these loans were put together on the commercial side as well as the residential side was because Wall Street bankers got fees. It wasn't to benefit you.

Let's say an investment-banking firm packaged a $100 million or $200 million commercial loan, at 95 percent leverage. They sell it to the secondary market, so a pension fund ends up owning it. The investment banking firm has taken its cut, in the form of a $2 million or $3 million fee. They are done. They don't care anymore whether the loan gets paid back or not. They're not in the loan repayment business. They are in the loan-making business—which means the fee-generation business—and they are gone.

Now, if you think that consumers are not paying the price for these debts when they go south, you are wrong. Just take a look at the last real estate collapse, that of the early 1990s, which we discussed in Chapter 4. The average person, in the form of the U.S. taxpayer, helped make all these Wall Street banks and private equity firms rich. When the FDIC took over all the real estate assets then held by savings and loan associations—a portfolio that ran into the hundreds of billions of dollars—these properties were then sold to Wall Street groups for as little as 25 cents on the dollar. A $50 million sale to a private equity group represented a $150 million loss, and that loss was paid for by the American tax payer.

Adding insult to injury is the fact that the players on Wall Street, the private equity guys and so forth, aren't paying much in the way of taxes. Stephen Schwartzman, the cofounder and CEO of the Blackstone Group who became worth nearly $8 billion when his company went public, pays a lower tax rate than a fireman in New York City.

When you understand this, you see that the system has taken advantage of the average consumer. So there's no need to feel bad. The reality is that today's consumer has been screwed, and now needs to think in terms of renegotiation. Rather than being embarrassed, consumers need to be angry about being taken advantage of. They thought there would be a system of fairness, one in which the consumer laws protected them. But they were wrong.

What is fascinating to me, in the way of public perception and the way in which the system works, is how someone on a corporate level can lose billions of dollars and suffer no personal consequences. Stanley O'Neal, the CEO of Merrill Lynch, earned $48 million in 2006. When he was forced to resign in 2007 after Merrill posted a quarterly loss of $2.3 billion and had to write down $7.9 billion in bad debt, O'Neal was rewarded with a $160 million retirement package.

Compare that to the small businessperson who loses money. The banks will go after him, sometimes personally. Why the forgiveness of CEOs at major public corporations? Why such a stigma for the individual? Why aren't you punished when you lose a billion dollars for your corporation, but as a small business owner lose everything when the business fails?

What makes it more insulting is that, in the case of the small business, the owner's money is often involved. In the case of public companies, the money is not the CEO's. It's public money, in the form of pension funds, or mutual fund money, or stock sold on the open market. And the system works by just lending more money to the corporations, or by paying off the first bank with refinance money from the next.

That is the way the system is designed. We tend to be hard on ourselves as individuals, but somehow believe in the hierarchy of the country even as corporate abuses unfold. We allowed the big companies to make subprime loans. We allowed the people who manage pension fund money to make millions of dollars investing in the repackaged loans.

Just think about it. The guys at Merrill Lynch are still living high on the hog. Schwartzman took Blackstone public, pocketed billions of dollars, and then watched as Blackstone fell 25 percent after its IPO, losing enormous amounts of money for investors. And what is he doing? He lives in a 35-room Manhattan apartment, and gave himself a multi-million dollar birthday party. And he continues to make huge fees managing

General Motor's retirees pension fund, and CalPERS retirees pension fund.

So he loses billions of wealth for investors, continues to live very well, and nobody blinks an eye. And yet we're panicked about our own home and the trouble we're in because one of these corporations sold us a mortgage at our expense. It was all done to retail us, to sell us.

So it seems that CEOs and their public companies get nine lives and that the stigma associated with bad business decisions is strictly reserved for the small businessperson.

Nonetheless, what you have to realize is that individuals—the business entrepreneurs—can also have nine lives. It is, in fact, rare that any extremely successful individual achieves his goals without first suffering at least some setbacks. So, it really comes down to a way of thinking. You've got to change your way of thinking in order to be rich.

Billionaire Mark Cuban, for example, went through a series of travails. Currently the owner of the Dallas Mavericks, Cuban started out after college as a bartender in Dallas, Texas. He then became a PC software salesman, but was fired from his first job in the business—for not opening the store on time while he was out making a sale. Rather than despairing, he started his own software sales company, which he sold eight years later, clearing $2 million for himself.

Cuban then went through a series of failures, unable to make any money. After five years of missteps, he started Audionet in 1995—a company that broadcast sports radio over the Internet—with just a single server and an ISDN line. It became Broadcast.com by 1998, and by 1999 it had 330 employees and $100 million in annual revenue. Shortly thereafter, and before the dot.com bust, he sold Broadcast.com to Yahoo for $5.9 billion. He has never looked back.

Real estate is filled with similar stories of entrepreneurs and individual developers who fell flat on their faces, especially during the real estate crashes of the past, but were able to come back. They didn't buy into the concept of embarrassment, even when they made big mistakes. The biggest and best example of this is Donald Trump, who today according to *Forbes* magazine is worth nearly $3 billion.

Back in 1990, Trump bet big—and incorrectly—on financing his Taj Mahal casino with high-interest junk bonds. By 1991 the project went into bankruptcy, and emerged only after Trump renegotiated with the banks. In that deal, Trump gave up 50 percent ownership in exchange for lower interest rates and more time to pay off the debt. A similar bankruptcy took place in 1992 for the Plaza Hotel (which became the Trump Plaza Hotel, naturally), with Trump giving up 49 percent of his ownership to Citibank. Likewise, Trump's 1989 purchase of the Eastern air shuttle resulted in a default and subsequent takeover by lender banks led by Citicorp.

When Donald Trump overpaid for the Plaza Hotel, some say he overpaid for it because of his ego, just as they say he did for the Eastern Shuttle, which became the Trump Shuttle (naturally) from New York. People say he had no idea what he was doing getting into the hotel and airline businesses. And when he realized it was going to take a long, long time for these properties to become worth what he paid for them, he just gave them back to the lenders.

But Donald Trump came back. Before the 1990s were over, he paid back some $900 million in personal debt and $3.5 billion in business debt. He reinvented himself as a personality and then licensed his name and starred in a top reality TV show called *The Apprentice*. Even so, in 2004, Trump Hotels & Casino Resorts again filed bankruptcy.

So if Trump can file bankruptcy on his projects, and cannot pay his lenders, and instead renegotiates with his lenders, why can't you? One could argue that Donald Trump shouldn't have gotten an American Express card at one point. Yet he now does a reality television show, and writes books on how to get rich when he was born with hundreds of millions of dollars. So why can't you renegotiate your loan? The answer is that you can, and should, work out a new payment plan or a deferral.

In essence, you have to change your mindset, think outside the box, and break the patterns. It's not a character flaw if you end up overextended financially because circumstances have changed, because interest rates have changed, and you can't afford to pay your mortgage as a consequence. Get over it. I would think it would be more embarrassing if you were someone who's inherited great wealth and managed to screw it up, like Edgar Bronfman, Jr., at Seagram's. He lost almost every dime of his family's fortune, the Seagram fortune, through one bad deal after the next. Seagram's, for all intents and purposes, has ceased to exist thanks to him. Now, that's embarrassing.

What is relevant here is that, despite the transparent behavior of someone like Trump, who is out to squeeze as much money as possible from any deal, people will still lend him money. The deal didn't work out? Then you're not getting anything. And yet he is forgiven. And, as I said, he's not alone. Look at Ian Schrager. He went to jail for tax evasion as one of the owners of the world-famous Manhattan night club Studio 54 and spent three years in prison for it. Now he's a pillar of the community in Miami and New York, the man behind the latest trendy hotels.

So, if Schrager went to jail and got credit when he came out, and if Michael Milken did the same, the rules clearly don't always apply. The fact is that if you're a minority and you go to jail, then you're screwed. But if you are a white American male, and committed a nonviolent financial crime, and you made people money before you went in—well, when you come back out, if people think they can make money with you again, they'll do business with you. That's the reality of the greed factor.

Donald Trump can still borrow money despite his bankruptcies in the 1990s because people believe it wasn't his fault, that he was a victim of circumstances. They are both right and wrong. It wasn't his fault that the Savings & Loan crisis sent U.S. real estate into a tailspin. On the other hand, no one in his or her right mind should have lent him the money to do an airline. What experience did he have? No one should have lent him the money to do the Plaza Hotel, either, because it didn't make economic sense.

That is the same kind of situation that defaulting homeowners find themselves in. Banks and mortgage companies shouldn't have lent them the money to buy these houses in the first place, and they shouldn't have given them adjustable rate mortgages. The high rollers like Schrager, Milken, and Trump got excused because they were victims of circumstances and so should you. You need to recover emotionally, and need to get indignant; you worked hard all your life, and you thought the system would protect you. Well, it didn't. If Ian Schrager can fail and come back, so can you.

America and the big corporate world have us feel embarrassed. They have brainwashed us to be afraid; this is how the status quo is preserved. But it is not shameful that circumstances outside of your control have made it more difficult to pay your home mortgage. Or pay your bills. You weren't sophisticated about the financial markets. You didn't have the benefit of all these analysts who projected the future of interest rates. People you thought you could trust sold you a bill of goods. It turns out they didn't know what they were doing. Time to fight back.

CHAPTER 14

Showtime: Dealing with Your Lender

*The first lesson in learning how to think (and act)
differently is how to renegotiate. Even if you have a bad
mortgage on a property you own, you have more
leverage than you think, even in foreclosure.*

Your lender doesn't want your house back. That is the first thing to realize when it comes to the messy business of foreclosures. Banks are not in the real estate business; they are in the lending business. What they want is for your loan to be repaid. They certainly don't want to own the property.

The reason why banks and other lenders don't want to take your property back comes down to dollars and cents. It's a very expensive proposition for them. According to a 2003 Federal Reserve study, the estimated losses for lenders on foreclosures range from 30 to 60 percent of the outstanding loan balance. These losses are a result of legal fees, lost interest payments, and property costs. In today's down market, you can add the accelerated decline of property values to that list.

So, right from the start, your lender is motivated to work out a solution with you that can avoid foreclosure. Most people are not aware of that, and the majority of foreclosures remain uncontested, right up to the day the family home is auctioned off on the steps of the county courthouse.

Now that you understand why your lender is motivated to negotiate, the next thing to understand is who that lender actually is. The first rule in any negotiation is to understand who's on the other side of the table.

In many cases the entity that owns your loan wasn't the original lender. When Countrywide makes a mortgage, what happens? They make the mortgage, they collect the origination fee, the real estate broker gets their sales commission at closing, and they're done. Then the mortgages are all pooled into a package, which Countrywide sells to the secondary market (just like Fannie Mae, except without the same quality or underlying guarantees). In the secondary market these securities are purchased by pension funds, municipal retirement systems, and so forth. These are the entities that actually own the mortgages. Then they hire a Wachovia or some similar financial firm to service them.

So, when you are hounded to pay your mortgage, it's not the mortgage banks that are calling or writing you, or even the ultimate owners of your securitized mortgage, it's the servicers. Just as the person who sold you the house has no long-term interest in whether you made a good decision or not, and just as the company that wrote the mortgage has no long-term interest in whether you do well or not, the servicer could care less. They don't even own the loan.

This is, of course, why we are in such a mess today. Mortgage companies like Countrywide are not in the business of making loans, servicing them, and getting repaid. They are in the mortgage lending business, and then the mortgage selling business. So they use less care and discipline than chartered banks or savings & loans, in which the bank is actually in the business of being repaid for the loans it makes.

I say this so that you have a clear conscience when it comes to dealing with your lender or their representative in a foreclosure situation—or any other situation where you need to play hard-ball. These entities have no interest in your success as a home-owner. Those who brought you to the dance have made their money and that is the end of their business relationship with you, and you are essentially out on the floor alone where the music has stopped playing. The owners of your loan are mean-while light years away from you, and the only reason they care enough to negotiate is that they're in the process of losing billions of dollars.

I like to think that real estate is an honorable profession, but many times there is not enough objectivity out there. The brokers are not always going to tell you the truth because they want to make the sale. Appraisers who appraise property don't get hired again if they keep appraising properties under the contract price, because then the loans don't get made. And the mortgage bankers are, as we said, only interested in moving your loan across the table like a poker chip.

Having said all this, it still comes down to the stubborn fact that you are in trouble, and whoever owns the loan, they, or their minions, have notified you that your home will be foreclosed. What can you do? First, in the spirit that forewarned is forearmed, you should know how foreclosure works.

The principles of foreclosure on your house are simple enough to understand. The details are a little more complex. So let's start with the principles.

Mortgage lenders, such as banks, are called "secured" creditors. They are creditors that have lent you money against an asset you have pledged. The most common secured loans are for homes or cars. The other kind of loan is the one made by unsecured creditors—credit card companies, for example.

In the case of your home, your lender has a lien on your property. This means that if you do not pay the money you owe, the lender can take over the asset that was pledged for the loan.

Different lenders have different thresholds for when they release the legal hounds that actually do the foreclosing. Before that process begins, mortgage holders will grant a grace period of three or four months. But once that lender's threshold has been reached, the case is handed over to the attorneys. They go before a judge and ask for adjudication that the loan collateral—in this case your house—go to the clerk of the county court for sale.

These sales are typically executed by public auction, but the property may also be sold prior to auction, depending on the procedures and policies of the court and the lender.

Once the property is sold, the proceeds are distributed first to the primary lien holder, followed by the inferior lien holders. Let's say you have a first mortgage and a second mortgage, the latter of which could also be a line of credit, home-equity loan. If you fail to pay either one and the lenders foreclose, the monies from the auction go to the first mortgage holder until they are completely repaid, then whatever remains goes to the second mortgage holder. If there were a third mortgage holder, they would collect only after number two was paid in full.

This, by the way, is why a lot of second-mortgage holders are not foreclosing, because if the sale price of the foreclosed house doesn't pay off the first mortgage holder and all the costs of the foreclosure they may actually lose money on the deal.

Now, back to timing. Most mortgage holders will give the borrower three months before foreclosure proceedings begin, some four. Then the lawyers prepare the case and serve the homeowner. This may take a couple of weeks or more; once the legal process is underway, it can be resolved in about 60 days, though in some states the process can take longer. The homeowner is now a former homeowner and is promptly evicted.

This timetable stays on track only if the homeowner goes down passively, however, and doesn't put up a fight. In fact, there are numerous ways in which the process can be delayed by the homeowner. How many ways? About as many ways as a girl can say no to someone asking for a date, as one of my lawyers puts it. The homeowner can claim that payments were actually made. Or the homeowner can claim that someone else was the actual lender, and hence the current collector has no basis. Or the homeowner can contest the foreclosure based on the lender's failure to take certain correct legal actions. Frequently these claims are only marginally legitimate; they can nonetheless delay the process for months.

Other claims by the homeowner may have more weight. In the current meltdown crisis, borne along as it has been by the sale of exotic and risky loan products, homeowners can allege malfeasance on the part of the lender, charging the mortgage holder with usury (a.k.a. loan sharking), coercion, or other unsavory practices. In the past many of these types of countersuits would probably have been dismissed as creative BS; in today's highly publicized mortgage crisis, judges are likely to be more sympathetic.

In the end, the debt remains, however, and most methods to delay foreclosure are simply that, a way to delay. If you can't make a deal with the bank, your house will be sold. Which can lead to another headache: What happens if the house is sold at auction for less than is owed the bank? This is not uncommon in a downward spiraling real estate market.

If your house fetches less than is owed, the lender can file for what's called a deficiency judgment. It's just what it sounds like: the lender can file a lien against your other assets—even your wages—for the difference between what they got and what they are owed.

If the gap is not extreme, lenders may simply choose to walk away from the deficiency. Otherwise you can protect yourself from a deficiency judgment by negotiating with your bank prior to the sale of the home. You can tell your lender, for example, that you will get out of their way very fast if they agree to forgo the deficiency judgment. Otherwise you can threaten to substantially delay the situation with a variety of actions, including some of the ones mentioned above. Another way to slow things down is bankruptcy.

Bankruptcy is something that can be filed by anyone in the United States. There are some institutions that cannot file, and some probate cases that prevent it, but by and large, any individual in the United States can declare bankruptcy.

There are different types of bankruptcy, but for the individual and for our purposes there are only two that make sense: Chapter 7 Bankruptcy and Chapter 13 Bankruptcy.

Chapter 7 is the straightforward approach. You list all your assets and all your liabilities, and you tell the court that you are willing to give up all your assets—which are then liquated by a trustee and distributed to your creditors—in exchange for being discharged from all you debts. What you are saying is: "I give up all I own in order to get away from all I owe." It's the ultimate starting over.

Now, there are certain wrinkles to the deal. For one, your credit will be shot for 7 to 10 years, and you can't declare bankruptcy again during that period. Plus, you can't get away from repaying student loans, or paying alimony, child support, or recent taxes. Pretty much everything else is forgiven, except for one big thing: You can't get away from secured debt. If a bank has a lien against your house or your car, they can still collect, and in lieu of collecting, they can still foreclose.

This will never change, by the way. Just as bankruptcy is something of a fundamental right for citizens, the secured loan is a fundamental right for lenders. Think about it. Without the ability to secure loans, nobody would lend you the money to buy a house. Think you can just go rent instead? Fine, But nobody would lend money to the developers of those buildings without securing their loans against the buildings. The whole country, our very economic system, depends on secured debt.

So, even though foreclosure is held at bay while you're in the process of declaring Chapter 7 bankruptcy, after the dust has settled your mortgage company will still be there, waiting, ready to pounce. True, the bankruptcy does get rid of all the other debt—which may put you in a better position to pay your mortgage—but it will only delay the foreclosure.

The other common type of bankruptcy for individuals is Chapter 13. Also known as "wage earner's bankruptcy," Chapter 13 can be filed only if you have less than $900,000 in secured debt and less than $360,000 in unsecured debt. This type of bankruptcy involves working things out with the creditors, and is appropriate if the debtor was faced with some calamity, like an uninsured family health problem combined with the loss of employment.

Basically, Chapter 13 allows the debtor to hold on to some of his or her property, in exchange for a reduced payment plan with the creditors—which the judge now has some flexibility to enforce—such as 20 cents on the dollar. The debtor emerges with a new relationship with his or her creditors, so to speak, rather than a complete divorce.

In Chapter 13 bankruptcy however, just as in Chapter 7, liens on the home—including so-called mechanic's liens, for work done that improved a home's value—retain their teeth, and must still be dealt with by the debtor.

So, does declaring bankruptcy do anything for you besides delay the proceedings? Well, yes. In the event your house is sold for less than you owe the mortgage holder, and you are faced with a deficiency judgment, that debt can no longer be enforced. With the house sold, this claim becomes an unsecured debt, and gets in line with the rest.

There is just one problem with this motivation, of course. If your goal all along was to avoid a deficiency judgment, then why not simply threaten to declare bankruptcy instead of actually doing it, and use that threat to get the bank to back off their deficiency claim?

Indeed, one of the big levers that bankruptcy offers the harried homeowner is the threat of using it. It then becomes a negotiating tool, a bargaining chip. What can be more refreshing than to tell a lender that you have no money at all, that you will be happy if they can find any money that you have, since you would love to use it, but that otherwise you will declare bankruptcy and muck everything up? Instead, wouldn't it be better if the bank just took over the deed and called it a day?

So, the best that bankruptcy offers those who are facing fore-closure is the threat to use it. If actually employed, its principal benefit—besides protecting you from a deficiency judgment—is to delay the process. If delay is the name of your game, and you just want to see how many months you can extend your payment-free stay at home, then declare bankruptcy. But it doesn't stop foreclosure, and it will take longer for you to rebuild your personal credit ratings afterwards than having your house taken away during the greatest foreclosure wave in decades.

Now that you are armed with a sense of what foreclosure is about, and what you can do to forestall it, the next step is to actually talk to your lender. It may not be the friendly face of the institution that made the loan, but even a mortgage servicer has the power to work out a solution with you, based on agreements with the loan holders. You need to speak with someone in "loss-mitigation," or whatever department is assigned the task of negotiating work-outs. They have leeway when it comes to the three most likely solutions: getting more time to pay the loan back; lowering the interest rate that you pay; or switching out of that deadly adjustable-rate mortgage to one that is fixed and won't keep escalating.

You may feel more comfortable doing this with the help of a housing counselor who can negotiate with lenders on your behalf. Such counselors are available in a lot of U.S. cities, and can advise you—frequently at no charge—on ways to delay and work out foreclosures. If you can't find a counseling organization from making local inquiries, you may be able to track one down through the National Training and Information Center, which provides training and technical assistance to community groups that protect homeowners' rights, or through the Neighborhood Assistance Corporation of America, a nonprofit advocacy and mortgage company that helps troubled borrowers get new, low-cost loans. HUD also has a list of agencies, which you can find on www.hud.gov.

The only problem is that because of the sudden onset of the current mortgage crisis, a lot of the community counseling agencies are backed up, if not overwhelmed, with requests. So you may need to hire a good real estate attorney; having one represent you also adds a lot more teeth to your threat to file bankruptcy, or litigate.

Speaking of litigation, that may be the ultimate tool in the struggle with your lender. Lawyers familiar with real estate foreclosures can buy you months with a smorgasbord of counterclaims, some of which we briefly mentioned above. In some states they can file a demand for a delay of the sheriff's sale, which can buy you months. In others it's a matter of finding the devil in the details. For example, the foreclosure paperwork may have the name of the servicing bank, and not the actual lender, and therefore can be contested. Or you may have been served foreclosure papers prior to receiving the proper notices by mail, and so forth. A good real estate attorney can pick through these particulars for you.

Again, these sorts of legal ripostes will only delay the foreclosure. If you want to take it to the hilt, you can sue on the basis of consumer rights violations, and actually claim damages for abuse. The argument in these cases is that you were defrauded into taking an unconscionable loan, one that did not inform you of all the consequences, and hence violated the Truth in Lending Act. Other grounds for such lawsuits would be that the loan was outrageously weighted in favor of the lender, with terms so steep, and so laced with phony fees, as to violate state laws of usury, or excessive collection of interest for a loan. You could also sue based on the fraudulence of overinflated appraisals—something that several homeowners have done against both Countrywide and KB Home. New York's attorney general, Andrew Cuomo, is suing Washington Mutual Mortgage for colluding with its appraisal company to inflate values, for example. In another celebrated case in Southern California homebuyers are suing their buying agent for misrepresenting the value of the house.

The downside to such lawsuits for you is their expense to prosecute, unless you can find a lawyer willing to take the case on a pro bono or contingency basis. In some rare cases, you may also be hung with the lender's legal costs if you lose.

Having run through the more aggressive alternatives to combating foreclosure, it is still best if you can work out a solution with your lender. If that's your strategy, there are a couple of things working in your favor right now. The first is that interest rates are dropping. That means that a request to reset your loan to a lower rate is easier to accommodate than it would have been a year or two ago. Another factor is the national mood, so to speak, and the various national efforts to save the nation from a foreclosure maelstrom. Among other ideas being bandied about is that of a moratorium, or a period of forgiveness. Lenders may be willing to write off a few bad months—or push those payments to the end of the mortgage—if that will get things back on track with you.

If you want to really think outside the box, you might consider offering to buy back your property from the lender at a discount. You would then need to finance this purchase through another bank, but if your credit is crackerjack (other than the mortgage issue) you might be able to own your home again but at a much better rate and with much more affordable payments.

Remember, your lenders don't want to own your property, and they don't want liability issues. They also don't want to let you off the hook for the money they lent you. Somewhere in between those two extremes there should be a formula that keeps you in your house, and with a national backdrop of millions of mortgages set to go up in flames, your lenders are more ready to listen now than ever before.

CHAPTER 15

Know When to Fold: The Time to Walk Away, and How To Do It

Sometimes it no longer makes sense to fight for a property. Then you need to know how to get out with the least possible damage.

Part of being successful in business is perseverance, the never-say-die attitude that eventually wrests victory from defeat, even in the face of extreme adversity. Other times you simply have to know when to let go.

This applies to real estate as much as to other industries, and it applies directly to the mortgage crisis we are now in. There are going to be investments that cannot—and should not—be saved. It's important to know the difference, and then to have the strength to act on your convictions.

Beyond the pandemic of rising mortgage rates that people cannot afford, the other big real estate problem today is the loss in value, the falling prices that are saddling homeowners with property worth less than the price they paid for it at the height of the bubble. It's one thing to try and save a house that's worth what you paid; it's another when you owe more than current value.

If, for example, you paid $300,000 for a house and it's only worth $125,000 or $150,000 today, and it's in Cleveland or Detroit, it may take another 8 to 10 years for it to be worth what you owe on it. Combine that with a mortgage payment that just went up, and maybe the time has come to walk away from the property, to work out a solution and give it back to the bank. While it will hurt your credit, it won't be catastrophic, especially if you work out a settlement prior to foreclosure. Future lenders will understand that you got caught up in the great mortgage crisis of 2007–2008, along with several million other homeowners.

It's still a tricky business to walk away, though, and you have to take into consideration not only what happens to your credit but also how to avoid a deficiency judgment, which is when banks come after you for their loss.

While you have to know when to fold, you also have to know how to fold.

The worst thing that can happen in a foreclosure is that your house sells for much less than what you paid for it and the bank decides to come after you for the difference. You can escape this debt by declaring bankruptcy, but that should be your last resort. Better would be to cut a deal with your lender ahead of time for what is known as a "short sale." In exchange for selling your property and giving the bank the proceeds, the bank agrees to forgo collecting the deficiency. You can also surrender the home to the bank in a timely fashion—that is, not fight the foreclosure and turn over the title—in exchange for their agreement not to pursue you for the deficiency. This is called a quitclaim deed.

If the deficiency is not colossal, by the way, then these concerns are moot. Most of the time the banks don't come after the consumer. They take the property and move on. Regardless of the size of the short-sale deficit, however, at least at this point you will not have to worry about the IRS. Previously, the feds could tax the amount of the loan forgiven that exceeded the property's fair market value. This was seen as regular income. As of January 1, 2008, however, there is no longer such a liability, thanks to the Mortgage Forgiveness Debt Relief Act.

Now, foreclosures stay on your record for seven years, so you will take a hit on your credit for a long time to come. There are two mitigating circumstances, however. One is what I said above, about future creditors being more lenient on a foreclosure that took place during these times. The other is that, as we outlined in Chapter 6, the FHA will guarantee a new mortgage if you have been foreclosure-free for three years and can show a reliable income for the last two of those years.

So, let's go back to our example. Say you do owe $300,000 on a house that is now worth half as much. And say you had an interest-only mortgage at 4 percent that jumped to 8 percent, taking your monthly payments from $1,000 to $2,000 per month. You decide to sell, but no one offers more than $150,000. You ask your bank to reset your rate to 6 percent, and they refuse.

At this point you have to ask yourself, is it better to pay $2,000 a month plus insurance and real estate taxes of another $600 per month for eight years (or however long it takes for the value to return to your home), or is it better to rent a $1,500 apartment for three years and then apply to buy another home for $300,000 via an FHA guarantee? Even with the FHA requirement of $9,000 down plus closing costs, you will have saved lots of money. More importantly, if we are still in a down market, you'll be buying that new home at a discount; it could be worth $400,000 or $500,000 by the time values fully return.

Most people are afraid of taking a step like this, however, and will struggle to avoid the embarrassment of foreclosure. Understandable, perhaps, but it may not even come to that. If the bank agrees to a short sale, then it will show up on your credit report as a settlement, not as a foreclosure. Even if it does show up as a foreclosure, you have to ask yourself: "Am I so scared of the appearance of a foreclosure that I'm willing spend the next decade of my life slaving away to pay for a property that's not going to make me any money?"

This is what I mean about having to think differently. Sometimes you should just bail out of a bad deal, stop paying immediately, and face the fight now, as when I told my bankers in Marathon that I would not pay them another penny. Get it over with now so you can move on to better things. Get an apartment, or rent another house, move your family into it, and give your property back to the bank. Let them deal with it. They're the ones who helped screw you over in the first place.

Now, don't take this advice lightly. You need to weigh things very seriously. If you can afford to make your mortgage payments, yours may be a different story, even if you owe more than your home's market value. If you can afford to pay, and this is the home you want to raise your family in, then go ahead and keep paying. Interest rates are going to come down, and you are going to be able to refinance and lower your mortgage payments. So, if you can survive, and want to be there long term, pay it. Over time real estate values will catch up, you'll get tax benefits along the way, and your credit won't take a hit.

On the other hand, if you know you are going to have a problem making your mortgage payments, and you know they will inevitably overwhelm you, then you are in a different situation. Or maybe this is just not the home you want to live in forever, and that even if you could make the mortgage payments it would mean giving up on a decent car or good health insurance, making your life a struggle for years to come. This is when a tough decision has to be made.

As long as you don't declare bankruptcy, and as long as you have a good credit history, keep paying your other bills and so forth, I don't believe they will take your credit cards from you, even if you lose your house to foreclosure. If ever there were a time when creditors would understand about people losing their homes it would be now. There is too much media exposure on the millions of people with mortgage rates ticking up on them. This is not just your problem, and it won't be the problem of just middle-class homeowners, either. You are going to see people at the high end having problems too. (And as I said in Chapter 13, if Donald Trump can go into bankruptcy on his casinos twice, lose his airline, lose the Plaza Hotel, lose the General Motors building, and then come back as the toast of the town with his own *Apprentice* reality show, then you can bounce back, too.)

So this is the time to do it. If you are in truly dire straights, defaulting and hiring a lawyer to work out a settlement with your bank may be your best choice. If you are struggling to make your mortgage payments, and you know the property won't be worth what you paid for it for many, many years, why spend good money after bad? Just give them back the property and move on, rent until you're able to buy another piece of property—hopefully at down market prices. That's where you'll make your money.

Index